A challenging, riveting overview of God's plan for a joyous, profitable marriage. Measured against God's clear instructions, a guide to an individual and for marital healing, fulfillment, and success.

—CHARLOTTE HALE
AUTHOR/SPEAKER, SAVANNAH, GEORGIA

This book will challenge you to take a closer look at marriage. Throughout its pages you will discover bits of humor, heart-searching challenges, and practical, biblical insights, which if followed and acted upon, will transform your marriage!

—BRENDA D. ELY, M.S.
LICENSED PROFESSIONAL CHRISTIAN
COUNSELOR, MARIETTA, GEORGIA

I believe this book will be a tremendous handbook, guidance, and direction for many couples committed to God's call for marriages of convenant relationship.

—REV. DIANE M. HALE
DIRECTOR OF UNIQUE BY DESIGN SERVICES, JASPER, GEORGIA

GOD'S MARRIAGE CODE OF CONDUCT

Blessings
Joy Callahan
John 8:32

GOD'S MARRIAGE CODE OF CONDUCT

JOY CALLAHAN

CREATION HOUSE
HOUSE
A STRANG COMPANY

GOD'S MARRIAGE CODE OF CONDUCT by Joy Callahan
Published by Creation House
A Strang Company
600 Rinehart Road
Lake Mary, Florida 32746
www.strangbookgroup.com

Unless otherwise noted, Scripture quotations are from the New American Standard Bible–Updated Edition, Copyright © 1960, 1962, 1963, 1968, 1971, 1972, 1973, 1975, 1977, 1995 by The Lockman Foundation. Used by permission. (www.Lockman.org)

Scripture quotations marked NIV are from the Holy Bible, New International Version of the Bible. Copyright © 1973, 1978, 1984, International Bible Society. Used by permission.

The views expressed in this book are the author's and do not necessarily reflect the positions of the publisher.

Design Director: Bill Johnson
Cover design by Nathan Morgan

Visit the author's websites: www.growinhealth.com and www.joycallahan.com

Library of Congress Control Number: 2010939121
International Standard Book Number: 978-1-61638-276-6

First Edition
10 11 12 13 14 — 9 8 7 6 5 4 3 2 1
Printed in the United States of America

Dedication

THIS BOOK IS DEDICATED to my late husband, Michael, who endured the challenges of his irreversible illness and the emotional sadness of not knowing earlier the revelation of God's truth for an intimate marriage. Michael was undaunted in his efforts to destroy the hold of this illness in his body and to restore our marriage to God's glory. Unfortunately, he ran out of time.

Michael encouraged me to bring forth the truth, by the Word of God, to address the *root* issues in our struggling Christian marriages. I applaud Michael's perseverance in his effort to destroy the works of the "enemy" in his life and in our marriage.

Michael's last words to me, the day before he stepped into glory were, "Finish the book."

Our twenty years of marriage, purposed by God, gave birth to this book.

Contents

Part V: Rewards

Acknowledgments

A SPECIAL THANKS TO EACH of the following people for living their "gift" and passion for truth, so boldly, before me. Their ministry and gift of communicating God's Word with personal transparency became my role model in revealing, handling, and expressing God's truth in this book. I am honored to have sat under their teaching.

- Joyce Meyer: author, lecturer, global outreach

- Dr. Mark Rutland: author, lecturer, evangelist, president of Oral Roberts University

- Anna Stanley: former Bible teacher at First Baptist Church of Atlanta

- Dr. Paul Walker: author, lecturer, pastor emeritus of Mt. Paran Church of God—Atlanta and Marietta Georgia locations, currently Director of local church development for Church of God in Cleveland, Tennessee.

Author's Note

HEARING GOD, AT HIS leading, on my four-year biblical research for this book, left my spirit saturated with His scriptures and scripture stories, along with many God-directed testimonies that are also punctuated with His scriptures. As the Bible often repeats the same scriptures and scripture stories to "establish a fact" of truth, there are several scripture repetitions in this book for the same purpose—to "establish a fact." It's God's unique way to make His voice heard. In stating His truths in this text for your edification, many well-known and not so well-known scriptures are repeated to underline these truths that are important to God. His desire is that these scripture truths will also become important to you.

Introduction

MARITAL STRUGGLES ARE COMMONPLACE today. Secular and Christian marriages limp toward victory, leaving more than 50 percent of American marriages headed to divorce.[1] How can this be? If there is a formula for a successful marriage, where is it?

I have a friend who I watched struggle with her marriage. She married a man late in life who had two previous marriages. This Christian woman had received the Lord as her Savior five years before meeting her husband. She believed she would never marry. She had her own struggles with her upscale retail shop and stayed very busy with business, church, Sunday school, and Bible studies. The Lord told her that a certain man who had joined her church would become her future husband, and this became a reality.

After an orchestrated six-month courtship and a six-month engagement, the two married in their church and were carried away in a limousine to a mansion for the reception, then off to Cancun for their honeymoon. It was a wonderful send-off. She believed her husband loved her, even though she didn't feel any passion from him, assuming it would come on the honeymoon because they saved their intimate joining for after marriage.

After the honeymoon, I could tell by my friend's empty eyes that something was very wrong. Over the next four years I could see her struggle to keep her joy. Meanwhile, her husband was diagnosed with an incurable disease and given strong medication.

At last, my friend faced her unhappiness with her husband. He was a good man who loved God and truly desired to have *this* marriage succeed. His method, however, was to take control in every area of their marriage. This, coupled with outbursts of rage and bad temper, made her feel like his emotional sounding board. His temper erupted almost daily. Nothing seemed to please him, and he seemed unaware that his verbal abuse was hurting her. It was very hard to understand how God could allow this to happen. Had she heard God correctly? Was this man really God's choice? Perhaps she had made the biggest mistake of her life.

The marriage continued to worsen as his illness started to advance but she remained at his side. At last, there was some good news, her husband was finally able to admit to his rage and temper outbursts and was delivered. What remained was damage to my friend's heart and to the marriage. As usual, she continued to put on a happy face because God chose this man to be her husband, and she was going to make it work. Still, she was not convinced she had made the right decision. Her husband's verbal abuse reduced to an easily irritated voice, of which he was unaware, but a tone she heard often.

He never talked to anyone else this way. If anything, he was a very friendly, social person and people enjoyed his fellowship. It was hard for her to understand what *she* did wrong to be treated so poorly.

For years, she grieved over the lack of passion in their relationship. Her husband didn't seem to be *there*. She couldn't feel his spirit. She couldn't feel his love, and she wondered if he was at all in touch with his feelings. It was like living with a demanding roommate who was always unhappy. Her frustration drove her to an intense search for answers. Christian self-help books and nine years of Christian counseling netted only small changes in their marriage. The major change had not happened! Tenderness and passionate love was never felt. Loneliness took its toll. Could this marriage be saved? The answer is a resounding yes! How do I know?

I am that friend.

Part I

My Story

Chapter 1

Who Is Joy?

OUTRUNNING GOD WAS NEVER a conscious reflection of my beliefs about God. After all, I did believe in God and while in high school, I sang in the choir at our church. Salvation was never a subject that was discussed in any kind of detail. My parents thought going to church as often as possible, two to three times a month and during the holidays, was making a statement of belief. There is a God. That seemed good enough for me. So by the time I was heading off to college, I had packed everything but the small, dusty King James Bible my father had given me at Christmas.

While at Florida State University, I became enchanted with the deeper meaning to human behavior. I found myself taking as many psychology electives as was permissible by my Dean of Fashion Merchandising. She cut me off after two years and insisted I take more electives in the School of Home Economics. I rebelled to her entrapment strategies. After all, I just wanted to be a fashion buyer, not a Home Economics teacher—sorry teachers.

So I turned my free time to reading astrology and the fascinating concepts of zodiac signs. My fascination grew, as it seemed to satisfy my thirst for understanding human behavior and how choices impacted people's lives. By the time I graduated with my BS in Fashion Merchandising, I was also armed and "degreed" with a keen understanding of astrology—to the point that within a five-minute conversation with someone, I could determine his or her zodiac sign. I was convinced that this newfound knowledge gave me the edge for understanding and connecting the dots of human behavior.

Reflecting back, I do remember my encounter with the Ouija board during my sophomore year in college. It was great fun asking questions and letting this "mystery force" spell out the answers. I could play on the board with most girls in the dorm, except for one girl.

The Ouija pointer literally wouldn't budge. I found out later she was a Baptist and deducted that being a Baptist must have somehow jinxed the board game. God must have had a good laugh at my folly. It wasn't until many years later that I realized just how close an eye Father God kept on me.

Upon graduation, I was off to the big city of Atlanta to start my internship at a major department store. I was poised and schooled for my buying position. My love for astrology was no longer holding my interest as it did when I first discovered its charm, so my next step was to enroll in metaphysical courses in downtown Atlanta. It was there that I was introduced to numerology, automatic writing, and aura reading. I had found my niche. Oh, how I loved psychology. (Somehow, I thought all this was a *form* of my beloved psychology.) Metaphysical teachings became so natural and easy for me to understand, which made applying them to the dynamics of human behavior a great asset—so I thought.

I left my buying job after thirteen years, in search of a deeper meaning to life and to expand my horizons. After many job turnovers of either accomplishing the goals of the job or boredom, I was frustrated with my future and my place in it. Church and God were never part of the *choices* I had in mind. I believed in God. I certainly didn't need to go to church each week to prove I was a good person. I wasn't cheating, killing anyone or breaking any of those other Ten Commandments that eluded me at the moment—like the one, "You shall have no other gods before Me." I am a kind, thoughtful person, someone God would love. He knows me. I say hello to Him every now and then. I try to go to church at Easter and Christmas. The songs sound familiar. I say the Lord's Prayer each night. So why was I running in place with no direction to my life?

In mid-December 1980, I received a call from an old girl friend who had married, moved away, was now divorced, and had moved back into my condominium complex. Karen had "found God." I told her how happy I was for her and that I didn't need to go to church each week to be validated as a Christian. Karen would not take no for an answer. Every Saturday she would call, "are you going to church with me tomorrow?" Running out of excuses, I finally agreed to go to her church. Perhaps this would put a stop to the calls.

Dressed to the hilt, fox jacket and all, I was ready to impress God with my visit to this very large, popular Pentecostal church. (I didn't know one church from another or which one stood for what, other than the idea that Baptists obviously didn't play the Ouija Board.) Toward the middle of the service, a man stood up and began to mumble words that didn't make any sense. I told Karen later over brunch that I was surprised a church of that caliber and size would allow a drunk to stand up and babble. That was my first encounter with the *gift of tongues.* You would think I'd feel right at home with all this sense of mystery.

I must admit it was a powerful service, in that I began to cry uncontrollably the moment the choir began singing. And it didn't get much better after that. Though I honestly don't remember the message Dr. Paul Walker was giving—I just remember the crying didn't stop. By the time we left the church, my eyes looked like a panda bear's, eye makeup everywhere, except on my eyes.

I agreed to return the next Sunday to convince Karen that she didn't have to attend church each week to be a Christian. I just had a bad start that's all. Well, it wasn't any different the second or third time I went with Karen to church. I believe the crying was even louder, if that was possible.

As we were leaving, I overheard a conversation between the people next to me talking about coming back for the evening service. I said to myself, "THE EVENING SERVICE!" After an hour and a half service in the morning, they go back in the evening for another hour and a half service! Do they ever run out of things to talk about? Or is it the continuation of the morning service? That seemed like a lot of talking and listening to me. But my curiosity got the best of me. There I was in the middle of three thousand people in an evening service. I certainly didn't tell my friend Karen for fear she would add this to the Sunday agenda.

The message was on salvation, which was intimidating. I didn't know I was lost, so why would I need to be saved? The anointing on Dr. Walker in handling the Word of God and clarifying the need to be "saved," I found myself saying the prayer of salvation along with three thousand people, as we stood and held hands. I repeated the prayer after Dr. Walker, confessing my need for a Savior, the Lord Jesus Christ, and invited Him into my life to be the Lord of my life.

I was emotionally drained by the time I arrived home. I crawled into bed at 11:00 p.m., much earlier than my normal bedtime hour of 1:00 a.m. This was a power-packed day for my emotions to process and for my mind to comprehend the life-changing decision I had made. What happened to me? As I laid to my right side, pondering the events of the day, I was looking forward to a deep sleep. I was tired. I would sort all these events out in the morning.

My eyes were closed but a few seconds, when I felt myself shaking with a sense of hovering over my mattress. What was happening? I tried to open my eyes—I couldn't open my eyes. I tried to move my arms to the side of the bed so I wouldn't shake off, but I couldn't move my arms. I tried to move my legs to hook on the end of the bed—I couldn't move my legs. Still shaking over my bed, I *saw* Satan standing next to my bed looking down at me with his gory eyes. I was confused. "What did he want?"

As a new believer of two hours, all I could remember was the blood of Jesus. So I tried to force my mouth open to say, " I put the blood of Jesus on you, Satan!" But as I forced my mouth open to speak, I began to hiss as if I was possessed. So that didn't work. Then I realized, through all of this, I could think. That area didn't seem paralyzed. So I said with my mind, "I put the blood of Jesus on you, Satan." And with that, I *saw* Jesus stand next to Satan, look him in the eye, and walk him out of my home. I quickly fell onto the mattress and then *saw* two very tall male, blond-headed angels standing like bedposts at the foot of my bed with their wings back towards me. I *saw* a twinkling, white sheet come over me as I fell into a deep sleep. I remember saying under my breath, "Oh, Lord Jesus this feels so good, just take me home with You," as I drifted off to sleep.

As morning broke and light filled my bedroom I was keenly aware that I was different and sensed a peace, I had never before experienced, engulf me. What happened to me last night? Was it a dream? No, it wasn't a dream, I deducted; I was awake through the whole experience. As I went about my day, I felt connected to a stronger force than I had ever experienced before. By 4:00 p.m., I called my friend Karen and told her "my story." She went hysterical! I didn't know that this was not a common reaction to being saved. I asked Karen the type of Bible to buy. It seemed everyone going to that church was carrying one, and the Bibles looked well read and worn.

So with the same zeal that I attacked anything new and spiritual, I was on a quest to understand what happened to me that Sunday night. Also, what did it mean to be saved, and why would that decision later change my heart and my desires? I felt the word salvation was a good starting place. With my new NIV Bible and highlight pen, I began my search in the Word of God. I couldn't seem to stop reading. I was so fascinated by the stories that Jesus told and the wisdom He used to clarify His points. I treasured His Word. That coupled with going to church Sunday morning, Sunday night, and Wednesday night—I was home.

My salvation and walk with God started the second Sunday in January 1981, and I have never looked back. I must admit that being stubborn and strong-willed has caused me to lose meaningful time with my Savior and Lord, Jesus Christ. But I am glad that one day is like a one thousand years, and one thousand years is like one day in God's economy. I am grateful that my life belongs to Him

About the shaking, that was God. It was later explained to me by a Bible scholar/ teacher, quoting Hebrews 12:27—paraphrasing—"I will shake you of everything that is not of Me, so that which is of Me, remains." Amen.

Chapter 2

Why This Book?

A FOCUSED SEARCH FOR ANSWERS, plus good communication skills, had always netted positive results for me—until I
got married. Almost immediately, I felt I was swimming in shark-
infested waters with no land or rescue in sight. I became fearful for
the first time in my life. There seemed to be no answer as to why my
marriage was so empty of tender emotions and intimacy. Even when
applying what I considered good verbal communication skills, I was
left sounding like his hard-to-please mother.

Years of Christian counseling for my late husband, Michael, and
myself brought about small changes, with many more questions than
answers. Then God took me deep into His Word and gave me revelation knowledge of His definition of marriage and why marriages, even
those between well-intentioned Christians, struggle to be fruitful. He
quoted, "My people are destroyed for lack of knowledge" (Hosea 4:6);
and He added, "Christian marriages should be the envy of the secular
world and they are not!"

Later, God showed me that He had ordained my marriage and
purposed this book. I had an awesome sense of His presence, and
I found a renewed self-confidence. His guidance and wisdom,
coupled with my strong desire to understand the cause of my roommate marriage, became a six-year romance with God. His Word

revealed passion, respect, and truth as vital ingredients for a healthy and holy marriage.

God aches for the Christian couple, masquerading as a happy and content husband and wife, while living in an emotionally empty marriage. He wants this mockery exposed and stopped. Unfortunately, this same lack of intimacy they express toward one another reflects, in direct proportion, to their intimacy with God.

God rarely participates in a marriage charade. As He says, "Their words are perfect, but their heart is far from Me" (Isa. 29:13, author's paraphrase). Thus, to measure the depth of our intimacy with God—we have only to look at our own marriage.

God ignited a passion in me that day; one that had me interviewing any married or divorced Christian who would talk with me. For nearly five years, I talked and listened to many spouses and discovered that no matter how long the marriages had endured, most stories were basically the same. This revelation only further fanned the flames of my passion to find God's truth to bring healing to these roommate marriages and restore the passionate intimacy for which they were designed.

God defined His objectives to provide a clear understanding of the mission for husbands and wives:

- Rules
- Roles
- Rewards

Truthfully, I was not excited about the word *rules*. I wondered if I could soften it a bit. He replied, "Would you drive a car without rules? Would you run a race without rules?" When He finished, I *love* rules! Understanding what God requires of a husband and wife gave me a clearer picture of what could be malfunctioning in a Christian marriage from God's perspective.

I have enjoyed the writing, researching His Word, hearing from God, and the interviews with Christian couples, who allowed me to speak God's truth into their marriages. And I have also enjoyed watching firsthand the changes this knowledge has made in me as a woman and a wife.

God requires Christians to be doers of His Word, not just listeners. For those who are serious about improving their marriage to the glory of God, let us begin to apply His Word to the broken parts of your marriage. I promise enlightening and soul-satisfying results.

The Mission Statement

Purpose

The purpose is building strong Christian marriages that reflect God's passion.

> Husbands, love your wives, just as Christ also loved the church—as He nourished and cherishes it.
>
> —Ephesians 5:25, 29

How

The Rules: Understanding marital goals, comes through knowledge of the scriptures.

My people are destroyed for lack of knowledge.

—HOSEA 4:6

Why

The Roles: Christian marriages are ravished by the same high divorce rate as secular marriages—60 percent plus. How is this possible?

Beloved, do not imitate what is evil, but what is good.

—3 JOHN 11

But I want you to be wise in what is good and innocent in what is evil.

—ROMANS 16:19

Brethren, do not be children in your thinking; yet in evil be infants, but in your thinking be mature.

—1 CORINTHIANS 14: 20

When

The Rewards: The time is *now*.

For it is time for judgment to begin with the household of God.

—1 PETER 4:17

When your day is over, what encounters meant the most to you? Who shares your joys and sorrows, your successes and failures, your laughter and tears? Is there someone who listens to your heart? Who really cares about your pain? God does.

Chapter 3

My Marriage

IN JANUARY OF 1985, God revealed to me that I would soon be married. Outrunning marriage proposals for years had convinced me I had messed up God's plans, so I was delighted with His news of my forthcoming marriage. *His* spousal choice for marriage would later become my wake-up call to understand God's purpose and plans for marriages and why they so often fall short of fulfillment.

My husband Michael was handsome, smart, and loved the Lord. He had a degree in electrical engineering and worked for the Space Program in Cape Canaveral, Florida. An earlier six-year marriage had blessed him with a beautiful daughter, Cade. Then he was a bachelor for ten years, followed by a three-year marriage that also ended in divorce. In March 1985, Michael received Christ as his personal Savior.

Exactly one year later, God revealed to me that Michael, a new member at my church, would be my husband. I chose to trust God with His choice and said nothing of this to Michael.

Although every single woman in the church seemed attracted to this tall, dark, green-eyed "George Clooney" look-alike, I said nothing. It was an exercise in patience, waiting for my first date with a man who had not yet been introduced to me.

We were introduced several months later. Michael invited me to our church's singles retreat, (which God strongly suggested I attend) and after the retreat, we started dating. We courted for six months and were engaged for another six months. It was hard to sort out my feelings for Michael. His qualifications looked good on paper, but there was a lacking. There was a sense of not being chosen. I discounted this to nerves of my forthcoming marriage and trusted God for a passionate marriage.

We married on June 6, 1987. On the third day of our honeymoon, the truth of my foreknowledge of our marriage was revealed to a very shocked and surprised Michael.

I should have known that God was up to something. This something would require my total surrender and obedience. I am now totally convinced at the time of my salvation, that I must have raised my hand and said to God, "send me."

Michael was diagnosed with an autoimmune mixed-connective-tissue disease in November 1986. Being the honorable man that he was, Michael took me to his doctor who explained, "as long as he takes this little white pill, he will be fine and fit to marry."

This pill was prednisone, and everything was not fine. Over the twenty years of our marriage, this autoimmune illness slowly consumed Michael's body, his ability to walk, to eat food, and eventually to swallow his own salvia. I became his full-time nurse, business partner, housekeeper, chauffeur, physical therapist, nutritionist, and part-time spouse. Much harder to bear than the physical stress and strain of daily responsibilities of attending to Michael's physical needs, was coping with the negative emotional issues that he could not seem to hear, see, or control. I felt I was never intimately married but was always a legal spouse with many responsibilities. This emotional loneliness was, by far, the hardest for me to endure in our marriage. I was looking for Michael to validate my life as a woman, but his emotional pain sabotaged any efforts to connect with me emotionally.

I tried everything physically and nutritionally to abate Michael's deteriorating health. I gave him ozone treatments, learned organic cooking, and numerous other health procedures during the last fifteen years of our marriage. Nothing helped and yet I still believed God for a miracle. I then began my search for the emotional root of Michael's illness, not only for the health of his body but the health of our marriage. His daily ease of irritation with me was evident in every part of our relationship, even as early as the first month of our marriage. Only I could hear this irritation in his voice, which further convinced Michael that my accusations were unfounded.

I became an avid reader of the Word of God, searching for answers. Frustration arose from not knowing the right questions to ask, coupled with a lack of understanding, as to which spouse was responsible for implementing the resolution, once it was found. Reading Christian inner-healing books helped a bit, but not enough, because the application of their information was still blurred as to who was accountable for making changes in the marriage.

I was unaware that I could not make certain needed changes in our marriage because those areas were not *my* anointed areas of responsibility. Consequently, changes were seldom implemented, or were aborted due to the lack of clarification. The journey to finding truth seemed endless.

In October 2002, while driving alone one evening, God spoke clearly to me, interrupting my heated and lengthy debate with Him on "will this loneliness in my marriage ever get resolved?" He stated boldly, I hold the man 100 percent responsible for the success or failure of the marriage! I could hardly believe what I was hearing. My immediate reply was that He would have to show me in His Word truths that supported this statement. Over months of tasting this truth, I found all the motivation I needed.

By 2004, Michael began to understand my research as he watched the boldness that God's truth had on my conversation with other couples also struggling in their marriages. Michael began working on his emotional issues in our marriage, but his sharp declining health hindered his thinking and concentration.

By the end of 2006, I had fourteen legal pads full of God's statements on His rules, roles, and rewards for marriage, along with the scripture references and stories that supported His points. He directed my reading. He would not allow me to read other Christian literature on marriages, listen to other speakers, or attend marriage seminars. He was very strong and clear on this point. God wanted me to have this information directly from Him.

Michael became my biggest supporter to finish this book. He also gave me permission and his blessing to reveal the struggles in our marriage—for God's glory and as a blessing to help others.

Unfortunately, Michael did not live to see this book completed. On November 21, 2007, my beloved Michael stepped into glory and is now forever with the Lord. He has received his healing in full. Three days before Michael was disconnected from his breathing machines in the hospital, he said, "You need to change the oil in the car, have someone change the filter on the furnace, and finish the book." Amen.

I grieved for all the dreams that would never be fulfilled with Michael. I believed God for Michael's physical and emotional healing.

And, for a marriage that would be the envy of the Christian community, let alone the secular world. Why God?

He softly said to me that I was only to have Michael for those twenty years, and that He had placed me in this challenging marriage for a divine purpose. So, living a focused life for Michael's care, handling a business, and managing a home, with limited time for social opportunities, left me a captive audience for God to pour into me His divine promises on marriage.

Chapter 4

The Roommate Marriage

I N A ROOMMATE MARRIAGE, a spouse never feels married. They never feel intimately one, just legally a spouse with all its responsibilities. How does this happen in more than 50 percent of Christian marriages—this feeling of living like roommates? You might think that in coming to Christ and becoming saved that we would divinely escape this travesty. Wrong! This roommate dance cuts through all boundaries. And with God's wisdom, I will reveal how one *learns* this dance and, more importantly, how one can stop the music.

An interesting note here: the wives in roommate marriages immediately understand this title, while most husbands seem to be baffled by its meaning. The curse that God gave Eve and her *sisters*— "And your desire shall be for your husband" (Gen.3: 16)—only fuels a woman's desire more. Therefore, when a woman marries, she is looking with joyful anticipation for the passionate oneness of intimacy with her husband. If the husband does not give himself intimately (cleave) to his wife, over time, her anticipation turns into excuses not to have sex or could turn into a charade of faking pleasure to keep the marriage together. Over time, the marriage foundation weakens and trust becomes an issue between them.

In fairness to husbands, I will clarify some common lies that pervade marriages. First, sex is not intimacy of oneness, per se. Intimacy results from a husband's intense heartfelt passion for his wife, by which *his spirit* draws her deeply and intimately to himself. The climaxing of sex becomes the final expression of his passionate desire for her, which then moves her into a deep intimate fulfillment of oneness. Second, the majority of husbands do not know whether they have *given* themselves intimately to their wives. Only by her reaction during the sexual act and/or afterwards does he have a clue that he achieved this intimacy of oneness. When he ask, "How was it?" He may often know the answer but is willing to hear the lie. Thus, the roommate dance continues.

The wives themselves become confused. Many think, as I did, that this lack of passionate desire has to do with something that they are doing *wrong*. Perhaps, I'm not skinny enough, pretty enough, I'll give him children, I'll give him a son, I'll give him my money, I'll go to work to help with his finances and then he will give me the only thing I want: him! Guess what? This lack of passion has nothing to do with the wife. It has everything to do with the husband's subconscious choice to be or not to be intimate.

One of the stories that God used to show me that the husband can chose to cleave or not to cleave is in the story of Leah and Jacob (Gen. 29:31–32, 34 and Gen. 30:15, 20).

Jacob was promised by his soon to be father-in-law Laben, the hand of his younger, more beautiful daughter, Rachel. Jacob was deceived. Upon awaking from his marriage bed, he discovered he was married to Laben's older, less-attractive daughter, Leah. After working out his wedding week with Leah, Laben also gave Rachel to Jacob as his wife, with the understanding that Jacob was to continue his care over Laben's livestock for an additional seven years.

Leah felt very unloved by Jacob's lack of passion towards her after this marriage charade was revealed. Thus, she voices her loneliness and rejection due to Jacob's lack of intimacy and oneness, which had intoxicated her on their first night together.

> Now the Lord saw that *Leah was unloved,* and He opened her womb, but Rachel was barren.
> —GENESIS 29:31, EMPHASIS ADDED

> Leah conceived and bore a son and named him Reuben, for she said, "Because the Lord has seen my affliction; surely now my husband will *love me.*"
> —GENESIS 29:32, EMPHASIS ADDED

> And she conceived again and bore a son and said, Now this time my husband will *become attached* to me [cleave], because I have borne him three sons.
> —GENESIS 29:34, EMPHASIS ADDED

> But she said to her [Leah said to Rachel], "Is it a small matter for you *to take* my husband?"
> —GENESIS 30:15, EMPHASIS ADDED

> Then Leah said, "God has endowed me with a good gift; now my husband will *dwell with me,* because I have borne him six sons."
> —GENESIS 30:20, EMPHASIS ADDED

Leah was trying to get Jacob to cleave to her once again, as he did the first time on their wedding night, when he believed her to be Rachel. But Jacob retraced his intimate passion, his cleaving, because of his lack of desire for Leah. Jacob was probably unaware that he was holding back in giving himself while having sex with Leah, an on-going obligation he felt required to fulfill.

An interesting point here: Leah could not have given birth to six sons without sex! So what Leah was complaining about was not sex, but the lack of passion and intimacy. This is the same complaining we have in today's roommate marriages because we confuse sex with intimacy. And of course we wives try to give our husbands anything, usually children and money, for that attachment (cleaving/intimacy) so that he will dwell (have oneness) with us.

Most wives never think to blame the husband for this lack of intimacy. Like Leah, who blamed her sister Rachel for stealing Jacob's heart from her, women blame themselves.

So, in an effort to make our requests known to our husbands, we ask them to be more romantic or more intimate. This statement is not understandable because our precious husbands are looking for the "to-*do* list," not understanding it's a "how-to-*be* list."

And this lack of understanding is where, over time, spouses give up and compromise to exist in their roommate marriage. Especially after children come along. The need for a solid home front plays a more important role than dealing with their non-passionate marriage. Therefore, the children come first, which is contrary to God's order in a marriage.

Here are some of the dynamics played out in a roommate marriage. Bear in mind that the wife is the glory of the husband and will reflect his actions, moods, and feelings back to him in like fashion. So depending on the husband's emotional posture in the marriage, the roommate dance can be a short quickstep or a long waltz.

Husband (initiates)	Wife (responds)
he parents his wife	she mothers him
rejects intimacy/passion	rejects sex
doesn't honor her as a woman	doesn't respect him as a man
self-focused	indifference
child-like behavior	whining
isolated from intimacy	loneliness
easily irritated	a nagger
treats her like a roommate	acts like a roommate

Because of our humanness, our desire for intimacy needs an outlet even in a roommate marriage. This need will be channeled through other acceptable avenues. Most often, the parent and/or parents become very pro-active in their children's lives, even after the children marry and leave home.

The children become the parents' focus for channeling love and getting the validation they can't get from each other. I say this in a balance: being a good parent does not mean you are a happy, passionate spouse glorifying God in your marriage. When giving an over-abundance of love, attention and nurture to your children, and/or grandchildren, and not to your spouse, it becomes "spiritual adultery" giving to others what belongs to your spouse. And we all know God's position on adultery. (See Matthew 5:27–28.)

If children are not available in a roommate marriage, the love/validation desires can be met with achievement in a job or career, as a tireless volunteer at the church or nonprofit business, or as a mentor to young people in need. Though these self-worth and need-to-be-needed desires are temporarily met from outside sources, they will, in the end, still leaves a spouse hungry for the intimacy and validation that can only come from their marriage partner.

The need for emotional touch and intimate nurture is so high on our list of feeling human and connected, that subconsciously spouses will adapt to survive. Some popular choices are: comforting themselves with over-eating, or becoming addicted to alcohol or prescription drugs to numb the loneliness. Or they fill their days with more obligations than can be handled daily, giving them no time to think or evaluate the emptiness in their marriage.

A roommate marriage does not have to be a hopeless dwelling place. To make the change to a passionate, intimate, oneness marriage will require honesty. The Word of God in James 5:16 says, "Confess your sins to one another...so that you may be healed." When a spouse can say, I am guilty of these outward negative actions, they are halfway down the road to healing.

With one sip of passion, you'll never take a substitute. The one great thing about an intimate change in a marriage is that the intoxication of passion gives you no recall of the lonely marriage you used to call home.

Part II

God's Definition

Turn to my reproof, Behold, I will pour out my Spirit on you;
I will make my words known to you.

—Proverbs 1:23

Chapter 5

Marriage—The Vow

But if you marry, you have not sinned; and if a virgin marries, she has not sinned. Yet such will have trouble in this life, and I am trying to spare you.

—1 Corinthians 7:28

THE CONCEPT OF MARRIAGE was established when God first presented to Adam his bride, Eve. When Adam first caught a glimpse of his beloved Eve, he felt overjoyed because she looked like him. He made this statement, "This is now bone of my bones, And flesh of my flesh; She shall be called Woman, because she was taken out of Man" (Gen. 2:23).

This marriage ceremony had no flower girl, bridesmaids, or maid of honor, but three divine witnesses: Father God, Jesus, and the Holy Spirit. Father God not only gave the bride away, but also officiated at the wedding with this one command to Adam, "For this reason, a man shall leave his father and mother, and be joined [and cleave] to his wife; and they shall become one flesh (Gen.2:24). This command is addressed to Adam alone, the only one equipped by God to fulfill this direct order. God gave Adam authority to create a marriage of intimate oneness. This same authority and responsibility is given to husbands of all generations, from Adam to present day.

God's wisdom has established this line of authority, which is knitted into the foundation of the earth. The earth and all its forces obey God's commands. He set the boundaries in place and told the seas how far they could reach, and even earth's unseen forces are given their commands.

A divine order of function has been placed into all the earth. These immutable forces move from season to season without man's help.

Adam was given authority to name all the birds of the air, the fish of the sea, and the animals on land. (I sometimes wonder about God's wisdom on the tick and the flea.) Thus Adam named them all, including his bride, Eve. At the point of Eve's arrival in his life, Adam was well established and grounded in his authority over his environment and now, his wife. It was Adam's choice as to how he used or misused this authority. Adam was very much aware of this anointing of authority that he was given—or was he?

The whole foundation of marriage was designed and fashioned by God to be a prototype of our relationship with Him. His design was perfect until man's free will kicked in, and the fall of mankind followed. No doubt, this makes Paul's insight more meaningful in 1 Corinthians 7:28, when he states to those wanting to get married, "Yet such will have trouble in this life, and I am trying to spare you." With well over half of today's marriages ending in divorce, the point seems well taken.

We then must ask Christian couples, who are struggling in their marriages, "How is your relationship with God?" Within lies the answer.

If we are "eating" the same spiritual food as the secular world and embracing their gods, we find marriage contains the same obstacles and the same death rate. God desires intimacy with us. He wants to be the only God we seek. He wants to be involved in our decisions, our choices, our dreams, and our fears. God desires a heart-driven communication between us not communication of rote lip service. God uses marriage as a metaphor throughout His Word to establish His desire of intimacy with His people. After all, God made us in His image, intending to have fellowship with us.

Now, to put the institution of marriage in the light of His intentions, we must understand that our heavenly Father is a literal God. He does *not* make suggestions. He gives a black and white directive of His rules, His roles, and His rewards—period. God has set into motion *all* the immutable laws before one came to pass. This means they operate with or without our knowledge of them. Most of us learned early in life about the immutable law of gravity. It's the other immutable laws we lack knowledge of that cause a troubled marriage to become a runaway train.

A *vow* is a voluntary pledge to fulfill an agreement. Notice the word voluntary. When one marries, it is a choice of free will that allows you to select your mate, then to legalize your marriage before God and the state. A vow is not activated until it is uttered, spoken.

> You shall be careful to perform what goes out from your lips, just as you have voluntarily vowed to the Lord your God, what you have promised.
> —DEUTERONOMY 23:23

A marriage vow before God is the same. He takes every spoken vow and oath you make, to each other, in His presence—literally.

> When you make a vow to the Lord your God, you shall not
> delay to pay it, for it would be sin in you, and the Lord your
> God will surely require it of you.
> —Deuteronomy 23:21

How serious can it be to break a marriage vow? Where is the back door out of a bad marriage? I have observed that a bad marriage most often is the result of not obeying the vows each partner spoke during their wedding ceremony. It may not be a bad marriage, but two people who have forgotten the vows they pledged to fulfill.

Eliminating verbal and physical abuse—which are legitimate get-out-of-marriage exemptions—the act of adultery and abandonment seems the only other recognizable Christian "out" for a bad marriage. To balance an understanding of the pain and separation of physical adultery, we must also consider spiritual adultery as a legitimate out.

Question: are there serious spiritual consequences to breaking a vow, made in agreement before God?

> When you make a vow to God, do not be late in paying it, for
> He takes no delight in fools. Pay what you vow! It is better that
> you should not vow than that you should vow and not pay.
> Do not let your speech cause you to sin, and do not say in
> the presence of the messenger of God that it was a mistake.
> Why should God be angry on account of your voice and
> destroy the work of your hands?
> —Ecclesiastes 5:4–6

How many husbands struggle to provide enough income to meet all their family's needs? What could be destroying the work of his hands? What vow was not kept? This could be one of the options to consider when seeking answers in a financially challenged marriage.

King David was a wise king because he understood his relationship with God, and he feared (respected) Him. He knew God's anointing was on him, that he walked in His favor, and that he could call on God for answers. King David understood the power of vows and oaths and their function.

In 2 Samuel 21:1–2 (emphasis added) we read:

> Now there was a *famine in the days of King David for three years*, year after year; and David sought the presence of the Lord. And the Lord said, "It is for Saul and his bloody house, because he put the Gibeonites to death…And the sons of *Israel made a covenant [vow] with them* [to live peacefully next to them], but Saul had sought to kill them in his zeal for the sons of Israel and Judah."

David understood the lack of fulfilling this vow passed through to him from one king to the next, because he understood God's authority and statutes. And King David also knew the steps of punishment that had to take place to lift this broken vow/covenant off his people. Once the punishment was executed, the famine stopped.

Likewise, when we make a marriage vow, the vow stands. When a marriage goes off course, perhaps a reread on the vows taken can point the way out of the unresolved issues. This is not the only thing that can adversely affect a marriage, but it's a good place to start.

Why do people want to marry? Is it for companionship? Is it financial? Is it for children? We know God said it is not good for man to be alone, and that we are to reproduce after our kind.

Could it also be true that we marry to have a *witness* to our lives? Having someone who will watch and applaud our living-out in front of them. We may hope that what we do each day will not go unnoticed by them, and thus validate our existence. We want to feel that our life matters, and their life matters. How powerful is this addiction to our state of well-being? It is quite addictive and can become the glue in most marriages.

This concept caused me to take notice of these dynamics in my marriage. When Michael died, I felt the loss of his witness over my life. The void of not being connected to someone can also be a great motivation to marry. Therefore, the valuable gift of marriage should be guarded against loss and/or damage. How well are you protecting your marriage?

Why else do we marry? Is it perhaps to discover the meaning of life? Perhaps it's to motivate our lives, or to stave off boredom or loneliness? Perhaps to find a purpose for our existence, or are we clueless about our motivation and simply give marriage our best shot? Let us become knowledgeable on this point: God takes marriage very seriously, and He takes what is vowed with our spoken words even more seriously.

God has formulated marriage for many excellent reasons, one of which is conforming us to His image. "Iron sharpens iron, so one man sharpens another" (Prov. 27:17). Nothing goes deeper into those locked places of our heart that has stored unfinished business than marriage. The process of making us more like Him takes a lifetime, requiring constant purging of our heart and our willingness to comply with the tools that God uses.

Chapter 6

Rules: Immutable Laws, Unchanging

> Do you not know that those who run in a race all run,
> but only one receives the prize? Run in such a way that
> you may win. Everyone who competes in the games
> exercises self control in all things. They do it to receive
> a perishable wreath, but we an imperishable.
>
> —1 CORINTHIANS 9: 24–25

THE WORD RULES SEEM very black and white, unchangeable, and without mercy. So when God gave me this part of the title, I was not delighted with the word *rules*. I thought it would scare people away. After all, if someone is living in a scary marriage, why read a scary book on marriage and its rules?

Well, God was mindful of my questioning. He said, "Joy, would you travel by plane without rules? Would you enjoy watching a tennis match without rules? Would you trust your government without rules?" Needless to say, when He finished His argument—I love rules! I feel safe with rules. I understand my boundaries with rules. I am glad He made the rules.

God has set down specific rules for marriage. He has made a set of rules for the husband and different rules for the wife: Surprised? I was. He also gave me a steadfast purpose in writing His truth with an anticipation of achievement instead of feeling apprehensive about hurting someone's feelings. He showed me there is no wiggle room with His rules for marriage. So if you don't play according to His rules, don't bother keeping a scorecard, for there will be no reward to list.

The scriptures that define the rules of marriage include:

> And also if anyone competes as an athlete, he does not win the prize [reward], unless he competes according to the rules.
> —2 TIMOTHY 2:5

> Those who love Your law [rules] have great peace, And nothing causes them to stumble.
> —PSALM 119:165

> Therefore, to one who knows the right thing to do, and does not do it, to him it is sin.
> —JAMES 4:17

Rules define the mission. Therefore, the mission statement for marriage is defined by its rules.

Once we understand each spouse's responsibilities in a marriage, it will often define the sources of strife and struggle between spouses. Ignorance of God's rules doesn't disqualify us from our responsibility in a failing marriage. It is like checking the oil gauge, water levels, or tire air pressure in our car. If this is not done according to the rules of car maintenance, we experience a bumpy ride. The same bumpy ride applies to marriage when the rules of marriage maintenance are ignored.

A word of caution here, *knowing* the marriage rules and *not* applying them, amounts to sin. "Therefore, to one who knows the right thing to do, and does not do it, to him it is sin" (James 4:17). Consequently, there will be a net loss of His reward and a loss of His favor.

When the wife performs the husband's rules and the husband the wife's, they sidestep God's intentions. God designed the male and female physically different so each can fulfill their individual rule as a spouse. The wife who tries to match her husband's physical pace complains of being tired. God made the male with 40 percent more red blood cells and 50 percent more brute strength.[1] (This is also reflective in sports. It's why women don't play football. Also in tennis, men must win three out of five sets and the women only two out of three sets.) God has given men the greater endurance and the greater ability to handle more of the physical needs of the family.

For example, if both spouses arise at 6:30 a.m., then the wife should be able to stop at 6:00 p.m. and pass the baton of responsibility off to her husband. He then would help the kids with homework and bedtime, while the wife would be able to rest and regroup.

By the same token, coming home to a clean house and a delicious dinner on the table would be relaxing to a husband who had to endure a hectic drive and overtime deadlines at the office. Making a home a peaceful sanctuary will speak volumes to a husband and confer respect.

You may say, "That sounds fine for some, but you don't live at my house." Oh, yes, I did. I am fully aware of the disappointment of being misunderstood, ignored, and having my intentions questioned. I know the pain of doing it all myself, without a compliment, or being taken for granted. Emotional isolation is a lonely place in a marriage.

If you taught your son or daughter how to play chess or monopoly you would pull out the rulebook and read the rules. You would coach and correct them when they fumbled over the rules, and with time and repetition, they would enjoy the game. They would understand that no one could win unless they played by the rules. Therefore, they are motivated to study the rules to become that winner.

God has given us His rules for marriage. He knows, as we seek truth, we will begin implementing His rules and become that winner!

Sounds simple I know, but there has to be a starting place for this journey into blessed oneness and intimacy. With each spouse doing his or her spousal part, success is in God's plan. This, of course, is not without some challenges and hard work. I'm not promising you a rose garden, simply the tools to start planting.

These *rules* will not bear lasting fruit in a marriage unless motivated by the heart. Unless our heart becomes involved in embracing the rules, the rote action of applying rules will not change a struggling marriage, let alone bear good fruit.

Put away your "how-to-act and what-to-say" list that you have memorized over the years. It is written, "out of the heart flows the issues of life" (Prov. 4:23). God said to His rebellious children, Israel, "your words are perfect, but your heart is far from me" (Isa. 29:13). Fulfilling the rules by rote will not bring results. Unless it comes from the heart, it's just a nice action that carries no intimacy. In which case, the roommate arrangement in the marriage will continue with isolation and loneliness its companions.

How do we get to that evasive root of why we don't have the heart to implement the rules? Lack of an open heart is most often at the root for the lack of intimacy in a marriage. The heart knows its own bitterness. God has a lot to say about the emotions of the heart. Expressions like, "let us get to the heart of the matter," means, "let us get to the truth." That is where this journey is taking us—to the truth.

This truth will set us free to embrace our God-appointed spousal rules, naturally and with gusto.

For the sake of clarity, I will give a brief definition of God's rules for the husband and His rules for the wife. These explanations will be covered in detail in the following chapters for the husband and the wife. Remember, the principle of re-reading the rules, so as to win, is the reason the book is formatted in separate sections for each spouse. Therefore, each spouse will be intimately versed in their individual section of rules and roles, and in addition can use their individual section as a personal workbook. Godly knowledge is a wonderful antidote to the lies we may believe about our marriage, our spouse, and ourselves.

Rules for the Husband

1. Cleave

The scripture that includes this *rule* for husbands is found in:

> For this cause, a man shall leave his father and mother and cleave to his wife, and they shall be one flesh.
> —MATTHEW 19:5, AUTHOR'S PARAPHRASE

This scripture is stated in Genesis by God, by Jesus in Matthew and Mark, and by the apostle Paul in Ephesians. As we know, if God states something twice in His Word, He is establishing a fact—should four times get our attention? I think it would be a loud wake-up call.

Please note in this scripture "For this cause, a man shall leave his father and mother and cleave to his wife and they shall be one flesh"—there is no participation required on the part of the wife to bring about this intimacy of passion (cleaving) in the marriage. Obviously, God has designed and therefore equipped the husband to totally bring about this intimacy and oneness in his marriage.

If the husband does not cleave to his wife, they are not emotionally "one," and the fruit produced is a lack of intimacy in the marriage. As designed by God, the wife has *no* authority or anointing from God to make their marriage one of intimate oneness. The wife is only the helper, and a helper is not responsible for the results. More later on exploring this design of God's and why it works.

"How can this be fair," you say, "you aren't married to *my* wife." Fair or not, the man is without excuse. God has not only equipped the man with deep emotions and authority to fulfill this mission, but God has given him a captive audience. One of the curses that God handed out to Eve (after they ate the fruit) is in Genesis 3:16—and God said to the woman, "and your desire shall be for your husband." Amen. Meaning that no matter whether the husband cleaves to the wife or not, she will continue to desire him, holding out hope upon hope that he will eventually give himself emotionally to her.

Pastor Henry Wright, from Pleasant Valley in Thomaston, Georgia, commented that "in all the many counseling sessions with women and wives over the years, it was because of God's curse on Eve that women are challenged with a desire for their husband. Consequently, women quite often stay in an abusive marriage way past the time that it would be in her best interest to leave."[2] This natural, God-given desire is only felt by the wife toward her husband. Is this perhaps why God does not have to command the wife to leave and cleave?

I know this to be true. I felt this emotional change on my honeymoon—that I was drawn with an unquestioning desire for my husband. The answer to this mystery was revealed to me in the course of my research, but I did not fully understand its function at first. Although it did cause me to reflect and reevaluate my attitude about the power and authority that God had given my husband over my life. Being in the dark is not a favorite place for me. It needs to be noted here that the wife's desire for her husband only comes into play after the marriage—it does not operate outside of marriage (more on this later).

To husbands who have not achieved oneness, intimacy, and passion in their marriage, be encouraged. Father God has revelation knowledge for you. Will it be painful to make these needed changes? How painful is your marriage?

2. Authority

Who's the boss? This may be the question you ask the first day of a new job. Why would this be important? Because you know this person has the authority to make your life successful or sad, livable or miserable. You may wonder if this person in authority knows the rules of their job and the rules of your job. So this person of authority can recognize your outstanding performance and grant you many rewards, accolades, and bonus points.

You also knew that you didn't want to displease this authority person because whatever they said would be your fate. And you surely wanted positive words coming out of their mouth when speaking about your abilities, and perhaps even your limitations.

How would the work environment be if you had a lazy, unkind, ill-tempered, self-centered boss for your authority? Would it be hard to treat this person with respect? Would you be able to brush off the negative words—spoken daily—over your work performance? Do you think this boss would give you hope for a good referral? Perhaps you are hoping for their transfer—permanently?

The point is, as the authority figure goes in a marriage, so goes the marriage. This is an easy deduction. What is not easy is—who is the boss?

This chosen-by-God, authority figure in a marriage—is the husband.

The husband may be unkind, lazy, self-centered and careless with hurtful words spoken to his wife and children. Unfortunately, the God-given power of this authority is not removed from the husband because of his unkind behavior. And these unkind actions and words will certainly impact and defile the wife and family members, for sometime to come. This authority is an immutable anointing from God and given only to the man. What a husband says and does will bear its good or bad fruit in his marriage and family. The husband will be totally accountable before God on how well he used or misused his authority.

For the husband to be ignorant of his authority over his wife and family would be like a foolish man who walks his family off a cliff, because he was ignorant of the law of gravity. So many Christian husbands are ignorant about God's rules, and reaped consequences. What He showed me was His protection to take the husband through his problem, once he admitted he *was* the problem! This transformation of confession does not come over night, but the freedom it produces is well worth the journey.

The authority mantel was placed across the shoulders of Adam. Therefore, it's anointing is down the male line to all generations. How can this be so permanent? Because God is a permanent God, and He has not left us clueless to this truth. There are many scriptures to anchor this truth that God has given only the husband this authority; and therefore the husband is responsibility for the success or failure of his marriage.

Most Christians are familiar with the story of Adam and Eve's disobedience in eating the fruit from the tree forbidden by God.

The scripture that makes this, a husband's *rule* is found in:

> She took from its fruit and ate; and she gave also to her husband with her, and he ate. *Then the eyes of both* of them were opened, and they knew that they were naked.
> —GENESIS 3:6–7, EMPHASIS ADDED

This is where we first see the husband's authority in action. When Eve ate of the fruit—nothing happened, nothing changed—their spiritual eyes were *not* opened. Yes, Eve ate the fruit in disobedience to the command given to her by Adam. This certainly was a bad thing; but the person who told her not to eat the fruit from this tree in the center of the garden was also the same person who watched her talk to the serpent and watched her eat the fruit. Adam did nothing. He did nothing to stop it. Adam had the authority to do so. Was he unaware of his authority until it was too late? It was not until Adam ate the fruit that both Adam and Eve's eyes were opened.

This authority from God is given to each male child at birth and will continue throughout his life. A man can use his authority for good or for evil. For the husband who does not understand or misuses his authority will harvest the consequences of his actions; and only he and God can rebalance his scorecard on the sowing and reaping.

I would like to highlight another truth to the story of Adam and Eve and the eating of the forbidden fruit. In Genesis 3:3, as Eve is talking to the serpent, she says, "but from the fruit of the tree which is in the middle of the garden, God has said, you shall not eat from it or *touch* it, lest you die."

First, God directly gave this command to Adam not to eat of the tree of the knowledge of good and evil (God never told Eve directly).

Second, God's command to Adam about the tree said nothing about *touching* the fruit.

> The Lord God commanded the man saying, "From any tree of the garden you may eat freely; but from the tree of the knowledge of good and evil you shall not eat, for in the day that you eat from it you will surely die."
> —Genesis 2:16–17

Perhaps Eve didn't *see* any change when she touched the fruit, so she pressed on to tasting the fruit. Curiosity can be a dangerous thing. Or perhaps, we see the first example of poor communication between spouses. Either way, the results of their decision to eat the forbidden fruit changed theirs and our futures forever.

We know by this story that God had given to Adam the authority over his wife and household, because nothing happened until Adam ate the fruit. God gave this same authority in another way to Adam. Actually, God gave it as one of the curses to Eve, in the presence of Adam, when God stated to Eve at the end of Genesis 3:16, "and he shall rule over you." This is the same *rule* that God gave Adam when He stated in Genesis 1:28, "and rule over the fish of the sea, and over the birds of the sky, and over every living thing that moves on the earth." God is saying to Eve, "I have given this same authority to Adam to rule and watch over you and be responsible; as I gave Adam for the animals, fish, and birds, for your safety and well being also." This lack of protective authority by Adam is further reflective in Eve's decision to be disobedient.

Although Eve was disobedient to the commands Adam gave about the forbidden fruit, with Adam silent at her side, her disobedience encouraged Adam to sin; and they both suffered loss because of Adam's decision to follow his wife's example. However, God holds the husband totally responsible for his use or misuse of his authority, and this authority is not lifted until his death.

3. Provider

The scripture that makes this, a husband's *rule* is found in:

> But if anyone does not provide for his own, especially for those of his household, he has denied the faith and is worse than an unbeliever.
>
> —1 TIMOTHY 5:8

The thought of living as an unbeliever is frightening. The husband is designed and "wired" by God to be the provider for his household. This could perhaps explain the husband's desire for money and the wife's for oneness and passion. How can these opposite desires work as one unit? Only God knows! Needless to say, the command is given to the husband in the above scripture and in Genesis 3:16, when God comforted Eve by saying, "your husband, shall *rule* over you, take *care* of you and *provide* for you."

As further stated in the curses that God passed on to Adam, Genesis 3:17 says, "Cursed is the ground because of you; in toil you will eat of it all the days of your life." Adam quickly got the picture of the challenges facing him to feed his wife and family.

Note in this story line of Genesis 3:17–19, there isn't a place where it says, after Eve had given childbirth, that she picked up a shovel and met Adam in the field to help him with his responsibilities to provide food for the family. It doesn't mean that Eve couldn't help with some of the chores in the field. It is just saying she isn't responsible to make sure there is enough food to feed the family.

This line of breadwinner has gotten blurred over the years in many Christian families. Although the breadwinner has the authority to delegate some of his job functions to his wife, it still leaves any financial shortfall or problems in the husband's lap.

As the husband brings home the income for his family, he may appoint his wife to pay the bills and balance the checkbook. No problem with this; she is his helper so we helpers desire to carry out the request of our husbands especially when both parties are in agreement to this arrangement. Here is how this "helping picture" should look. Once the wife has paid the bills, should she find she has more bills then money; she puts the checkbook and unpaid bills on her husband's desk, awaiting further instructions.

A wise husband would say to his wife, when initiating this policy with the family income, "When you have paid all the bills you can with the income I give you, just put any unpaid bills with the checkbook on my desk. I will take care of it. I will clear up the unpaid bills."

Therefore, there is no sweat on Eve's brow. In Genesis 3:19, God said to Adam, "By the sweat of your face you will eat bread."

The good news is that God has equipped each male with the gifts, talent, and ability to provide for his wife and family and then some. God never requires anything of us that He hasn't first given us the ability to do. Now it may feel like He is stretching our tent pegs, but that is just like God to reveal to us, in our trials and challenges, His greatness in His provision for that mission. Likewise, He always makes a way for each husband to provide for his wife and family. That's a promise He gives us as His children. He has a thousand cattle (profitable opportunities) on a hill for your supply.

Rules for the Wife

Helper/Companion

The scripture that makes it a wife's *rule* is:

> Then the Lord God said, It is not good for the man to be alone; I will make him a *helper* suitable for him.
> —GENESIS 2:18, EMPHASIS ADDED

> And the Lord God fashioned into a woman the rib which He had taken from the man, and brought her to the man.
> —GENESIS 2:22

And Adam said *wow*!

> This is now bone of my bones, and flesh of my flesh; and She shall be called Woman, because she was taken out of Man.
> —GENESIS 2:23

Helper

This should be a natural heart's desire for a wife, not only to be her husband's helper but also his companion. This would allow the husband to know that someone is watching his back, someone who has a vested interest in his well-being. This person, above all others, should be his wife.

Most wives perform this *rule* without much effort. I know this was true in my marriage. From the moment I was married, I had an innate knowledge of what was required of me.

A spiritual knowing, if you please. It seemed very natural to help my husband with his choices and decisions, as it pertained to our marriage and our family's well- being.

The caution with this is that the helper's function needs to stay in its boundaries. Sounds easy, but it is not always that way. Unsolicited advice often appears controlling, and not necessarily the best way to help our husbands.

Being the helper does not mean we help our husbands understand how poorly they perform their rules. It is tempting, but it bears poor fruit in the marriage. The best rule for a wife is to wait until asked to help and also be willing to let "the glass fall off the table."

For some people, experience is still the best teacher and this includes our husbands. Give them ample room for this learning curve.

Companion

This is one of a wife's favorite postures. We wives want to know everything our husbands have done that day. We want it all. Not so much to analyze their day, but for the intimacy of companionship. In

Webster's Dictionary, one of the definitions of the word *conversation* is intercourse. And one of the definitions of the word "intercourse" is conversation. Good companionship and communication are very important to the health of a marriage.

Desires/Intimacy

The scripture that defines this second *rule* for the wife is found in:

> In pain you will bring forth children; yet your desire will be
> for your husband.
> —GENESIS 3:16

Many years ago, I heard a Texan pastor say; "If God didn't give the wife a desire for her husband, she would never have children because of childbirth pain." This may or may not be God's intention here. I do know that desiring your husband is very real—whether you have children or not.

This desire for intimacy on the wife's part is a never-ending feeling. It defines a woman. She desires to be validated as a woman by her husband, which is only accomplished through intimacy, not sex. Sex, most often, is an expression of a physical need. It does not always require intimacy and passion to be achieved. When true oneness happens, the sexual part is climaxed and enhanced because of the passionate intimacy, which takes this experience of oneness to a higher level. The wife is the *open flower* (desiring her husband), waiting for the oneness/intimacy from her husband. If the husband cannot bring his passion for her into their marriage, then intimacy becomes just sex.

This is where we women learn to pray best—in the trenches. Berating a husband for his lack of intimacy will not bring the results women are seeking. Once intimacy is understood, and corrections are made by the *responsible* spouse in the marriage, then the marriage becomes grounded in new expressions of passion, and everyone is a winner—including God. Be encouraged in knowing that God will not only reveal the source of the problem for the lack of intimacy in the marriage but He will give the solution.

Childbirth

Giving birth to children is a blessing from God.

> Behold, children are a gift of the Lord; The fruit of the womb is a reward.
> —Psalm 127:3

Having never given birth to a child has grieved me greatly. The choices I made for outrunning marriage in my early years redefined my womanhood. Even though I pride myself on being a wonderful aunt to my three nephews and two nieces, the phone never rings on Mother's Day, and rightfully so, I am not their mother.

I applaud all you mothers who are reading this book. What a selfless act to lay your life so close to the line of death to bring forth a child. What a commitment to raise a child to his or her adult age. The nine months leading up to childbirth foreshadow the experiences yet to be embraced with their awaiting challenges. Be blessed in your motherhood.

Submit: subject to the husband's authority

The scripture that makes submission the wife's *rule*, is found in:

Wives be *subject* to your husband, as is fitting in the Lord.
—COLOSSIANS 3:18, EMPHASIS ADDED

Wives be subject to your own husbands, as to the Lord.
—EPHESIANS 5:22

But as the church is *subject* to Christ, so also the wives ought to be (*subject*) to their husbands in everything.
—EPHESIANS 5:24, EMPHASIS ADDED

Webster's Dictionary defines "subject to" as: being under the power or rule of another; liable; dependent.

I believe what God is saying to wives, and has said specifically to me, is that this statement of being subject is reciprocal to God's command to Adam in stating his authority to rule over Eve. God has so designed the woman to be dependent on her husband, and she needs to rest and be subject to his authority over her care, safety, and well-being.

This sounds like a neat package from God. As the husband uses his authority to assure his wife that he can care for her and that she is safe with him, she can sigh and rest in his protective covering over her life and lovingly submit to his directives in his ruling over her and their family.

Because of this authority God has given the husband to rule his wife and family, it will bear fruit of harmony or disharmony in the family unit, depending on how skillfully the husband uses or abuses his authority. If the wife cannot be subject to her husband, then she has to look back to her authority figure, the husband, as to why there is disharmony in the marriage. What a husband *sows* into his wife's life, this he shall reap.

> An excellent wife, who can find? For her worth is far above jewels. The heart of her husband trusts in her, And he will have no lack of gain.
> —PROVERBS 31:10–11

Note that the heart of the husband trusts in his wife. Therefore, she can handle all the chores and challenges she faces in daily life with confidence, bringing harmony and comfort to her family. The husband must *first* trust his wife. The scripture is not saying,

"Once the wife proves herself worthy by her husband's standards, *then* he will trust her." For a correct understanding of this scripture, first comes the husband's trust in his wife, then she does him good and not evil all the days of her life. Her submission to her husband is in direct proportion to his care of her emotional well-being and safety. The wife's behavior is a picture, good or bad, of how well the husband is handling his authority over her. Wives should pray for their husbands in this area. Some husbands may have had authority and submission displayed abusively toward them in their childhood. Therefore, they know no other method of handling their authority except that which they were exposed to in their formative years. With this knowledge, we can give grace. This is the same grace our heavenly Father gives us daily. Let us therefore, be mindful of the plank in our own eye. Praying for our husband may not be the shortest route to resolution but it is most effective, especially when we do not lose hope when doing what is right, according to what is acceptable behavior from God.

As He forms us into His image, "Iron sharpens iron, so one man sharpens another" (Prov. 27:17). Nothing goes deeper into those locked places of our heart, which have stored unfinished business, than marriage. The process of making us more like Him takes a lifetime, requiring constant purging of our heart and our willingness to comply with the tools that God uses.

Chapter 7

Roles: Attitude of the Heart

He who hates disguises it with his lips, but he lays up
deceit in his heart.

—Proverbs 26:24

G OD HAS FURTHER DEFINED the *rules* by explaining the *roles*
each husband and wife will need to understand for success
in their marriage. We are, therefore, without excuses. We no longer
can say, "I didn't know that was my job." Let us not get anxious. One
major hallmark of God is that whatever He requires of us, He has
already equipped us to perform.

Sometimes the understanding of what He requires of us in our
individual marital role can be confusing and frustrating. This lack
of understanding, coupled with the role models we grow up with,
conflicts with God's objectives for a healthy marriage, leaving us
guessing as to the appropriate actions for us to take. Grasping the full
scope of our role, *Webster's* defines the word *role* as "an assigned or
assumed character."

So, as I understand this definition, when I marry, I am assigned the
role of husband or wife and therefore, I am to assume that character
(role).

God Defines Roles

Let us begin with a brief explanation of the *role* of a husband and the *role* of a wife. These character roles will be discussed in greater detail in the individual chapters that follow.

Role of the husband: love, honor, protect

Lover

The swooning magnetism of Prince Charming and Casanova pales in comparison to the anointing and gifting that God gives a husband as a "lover." How wonderful is that!

The scripture that makes lover the husband's *role* is:

> Husbands, *love your wives,* just as Christ also loved the church and gave Himself up for her .... for no one ever hated his own flesh, but *nourishes and cherishes* it, just as Christ also does the church.
>
> —EPHESIANS 5:25, 29

This scripture is very clear, straightforward, and uncomplicated. There should be no problem with this role of lover for a husband, until he finds out that his role as a *lover* has less to do with sex and more to do with intimacy. I have found this fact to be true in my marriage and with other married couples that were part of my four-year study. In dealing with intimacy in marriage, the most consistent finding for the failure of the husband to be a passionate, intimate lover is that he doesn't love himself, and therefore, is unable to love his wife. Rejection of intimacy toward his wife often is not due to her behavior, but is more likely due to his lack of intimate validation growing up.

A note of caution here, a self-centered husband does not mean he loves himself. It just means he is trying to validate his non-validated life. There is a solution to this kind of pain.

> So husbands ought also to love their own wives as their own bodies. He who loves his own wife loves himself.
> —EPHESIANS 5:28

Conversely, the husband who does not love himself is unable to love his wife.

So far, the scoring on my personal survey is very high for women who complained of their husbands' lack of passionate intimacy. They confirmed to me, to the best of their knowledge, that their husbands were not adequately loved growing up. I understood this truth all too well. I grieved for my late husband Michael's lack of nurturing in his formative years and saw firsthand the emotional toll it had on him. I am his third wife. His first two wives divorced him after rather short marriages. Not having a relationship with God at the time, only added to Michael's lack of understanding as to where he went wrong in his first and second marriages.

As Michael came to understand God's truth and requirements for a husband, he was very grieved over the insensitive way he treated his former wives. He wrote letters to them apologizing for his negative behavior, his temper, and for the loneliness he created in their marriages. How different Michael's life would have been if he'd had a relationship with God earlier in life and had an understanding of His marital wisdom.

Is there a hope? Is there a God? *Yes*! Because God's truth, when applied, will always give us freedom from the sin that so easily entangles us. Thus, be encouraged that the taste of victory in your marriage is obtainable. That's a promise.

No one is more anointed or equipped by God to be the lover in the marriage than the husband. God has designed the husband for this role, to bring passion and intimacy to his wife, while cherishing her with tender, loving nurture.

I am very sorry for the loneliness that some husbands felt growing up in their family unit. I have heard it said by counselors, "They love the way they were loved." Fortunately, God has a better plan to redeem those years lacking passionate validation. Husbands deserve to feel the passion of their soul and the warmth of that passion, reflected back over them from their wife. We serve a passionate God. He is not lukewarm. He made you and designed you for His fellowship in His likeness with a heart capable of great passion!

Honor

The scripture that makes honor the husband's *role* is found in:

> You husbands likewise, live with your wives in an understanding way, as with a weaker vessel, since she is a woman; and *grant her honor* as a fellow heir of the grace of life, so that your prayers may not be hindered."
>
> —1 PETER 3:7

When one thinks of the word *honor*, a mental picture emerges of a person in a humble posture. Or the posture of a soldier giving honor to his commanding officer. To me, the word *honor* means much more than respect, although that is one of the words that *Webster's Dictionary* uses to define the word *honor*: outward respect and reverence.

Husbands need to be mindful of what this scripture, 1 Peter 3:7, requires of them and the consequences of their disobedience. Answers to their prayers will be delayed due to dishonor they show their wife. There is also another scripture that carries a very similar message and promise. It is the fifth commandment: "Honor your father and mother that your days may be prolonged in the land which the Lord your God gives you, so that everything will go well for you."

In any area in which we don't honor God, things will not go well for us. In dishonoring your wife, your marriage will not go well and your prayers (in any area of your life) will be ignored. The husband may not *see* this dynamic going on in his marriage. There is, however, one person who can give him the answer, and that is his wife.

Let me give you an example of a couple that was struggling in their marriage. In a telephone conversation with the husband, Steve, I asked, "Let me hear how you both are doing." Steve blurted out, "I wish Renee would respect me." I told him to hold the phone while I called Renee. My only question to her was, "Does Steve respect and honor you?" Her immediate answer was a loud and firm. "No, he doesn't." It's a painful reflection.

And so I say to husbands: understanding your role to honor your wife is always a good place to start the healing process in a struggling marriage. A good marriage is not built overnight, nor has a bad marriage been destroyed overnight. The choice is up to you. Yes, there can be obstacles to actually putting this honoring gesture into practice. Reading this book, detailing God's truths on marriage rules, roles, and rewards, is a good starting place. I applaud your efforts to seek God's face and, together with Him, refashion your marriage into a treasure of great worth. You are very capable.

Protector

There are endless stories in the Word of God that tell of the many courageous acts of husbands who protected their family from harm and danger. The battlefield is a little different today, but the principles haven't changed. With each generation, there is a new set of challenges in protecting the wife and family from harm. This does not, however, relieve husbands of their responsibility in this area. Some wives tell me they feel they are "sleeping with the enemy."

Webster's Dictionary defines *protect*: to shield from harm; to guard.

The scripture that makes *protect* a husband's *role* is found in Mark 3:27:

> But no one can enter the strong man's house and plunder his property unless he first binds the strong man and then he will plunder his house.

So how does this husband's role of protector get so misunderstood and mistranslated into everyday living? And why do wives feel so unprotected? If I had to rank the sighs I get from wives, one of the loudest comes when I ask them: "How would you feel if your husbands were a total blanket of protection over your life?" The sighing would begin. "Oh, how wonderful is that," they would say. Some husbands may think: "Where is *my* blanket of protection?" Herein lies the problem. The husband can only bring to his family what was given to him growing up. If the young boy didn't see or feel his father's protection over him and the family, insecurity and fear quite likely become early companions.

Note that the scripture quoted above is referring to the strong man—the husband, who is protecting everything that belongs to him that is under his authority. He is protecting his wife, family, and the possessions on which his family relies for survival and safety. The hindrance to this is the inability of the husband to stay unbound from the enemy. Note that the enemy (usually Satan) intends to bind the husband, not the wife. Satan knows if he captures the person of authority, he gets the *whole* family. That is a big concept to ponder. "Just how does that work?"

The enemy's strategy is to find those unhealed emotional wounds and unresolved sin areas in the husband. Therefore, giving Satan legal access to bind, render powerless, and destroy the marriage by capturing the husband, along with his total family unit. For example, if the husband has unhealed issues with pornography, fear, rejection, shame, lack of manhood validation, etc., the enemy will stir up trouble in these areas to adversely affect the marriage. When the husband falls, the family is left helpless and unprotected. Yes, a strong wife can pick up the pieces and bridge the gap in the marriage, usually for the children's sake. But it can't become a marriage that reflects God's intentions. Thus we see role reversals where the wounded husband "parents" his wife and the wife "mothers" him in response. And the roommate dance continues.

The one who is called to protect the family is the husband. He is designed by God to fulfill this commission and to carry it out almost effortlessly. The protection's weakest link is the emotional wounds of the husband. We will address this and make suggestions to this dilemma later in the book. God always makes a way when there seems to be no way. Knowing and accepting responsibility for the lack of protection over your wife is half the battle—the victory is half won.

Role of the wife: respond, obey, respect

Responder

The scripture that makes *respond* a wife's *role* is:

> But the woman is the glory of the man.
> —1 Corinthians 11:7

What a wonderful picture of "reflecting" the husband. As you perhaps remember the story of Moses when he would visit with God on Mt. Sinai and the glory of being in God's presence would shine brightly on Moses' face. At some point, he even wore a scarf over his face so as not to frighten people with this bright reflection.

The natural role of the wife is to reflect back to her husband—him. This was a hard principle for me to truly comprehend. A clearer understanding of this would be when the husband doesn't honor the wife. As a woman, the wife will reflect disrespect to her husband, as a man. I saw this dynamic of reflecting in my own marriage. Now, I finally had a name for it, an answer as to its source.

As God would have it, I had the opportunity to test this principle of "responder." I was attending a businesswoman's dinner function, where each person brought her favorite dish and spouse, if they had a spouse.

A story

Sandy arrived late with her husband walking sheepishly behind her. She exclaimed in a loud voice, "Anyone want a husband? You can have mine!" This dialogue went on all evening. I grieved for her unflattering reflection of a scorned wife.

The next day, I felt that I needed to confront her on her outspoken, childish behavior. After all, she made it very apparent in so many of our business meetings that she is a strong Christian believer operating in several spiritual gifts.

I said to myself, "Let's try out God's principle—that the wife's reaction toward her husband is a *reflection* of how he is treating her." When she answered the phone, I asked immediately, "Sandy, what did your husband do to you that caused you to act with such harshness and unkindness toward him?" Without hesitation, she told me that he had been verbally abusive to her throughout their thirty-five years of marriage. That he also would always pick a fight with her when in route to a social event. Was I surprised! Later, I gave my applause to Father God. He will tell us everything if we just listen.

So the role of the wife is the responder, the husband's role is the initiator. This is a great barometer for the husband when handled correctly. He can then see himself in his wife's reflection. If he doesn't like the reflection, he has the authority to change it.

Healing the Masculine Soul by Gordon Dalbey states, "Once the man's been healed emotionally the wife is healed automatically."[1] Wouldn't this take some pressure off our Christian counselors? They would only have to work with the husbands. I see that smile.

Obedience

The scriptures that make *obedience* the wife's *role* is:

> Obey your leaders (husband), and submit to them; for they keep watch over your souls, as those who will give an account.
> —HEBREWS 13:17

> Thus Sarah obeyed Abraham, calling him lord, and you have become her children if you do what is right without being frightened by any fear.
> —1 PETER 3:6

OK ladies, this is where we really have to trust that God knows what He is requiring of us. My personal observation: If you have struggled with obedience towards your parents, to that same degree you will struggle with obedience in your marriage.

Now let me assure you that God is very mindful of your abusive husband and the escape clause is found in the second scripture mentioned above: "If you do what is right without being frightened by any fear." The translation here is saying that it would be difficult to be obedient to a husband you felt would not do what is right by you and cause you fear. You would have to re-evaluate the level of obedience that you could commit to, especially if children are involved.

Obedience is a wonderful posture and state of being for a wife, especially if the husband is fulfilling his roles of protection and love. This may not always be the case. Let's be obedient where we can in the healthy areas of our marriage. Choose your words wisely when speaking to your husband. Be mindful that any unkind words may come back to you from a mouth that has "authority" (Numbers 30).

You know well the areas in your relationship that bring strife. Let wisdom guide your choices of communication with your spouse.

Let prayer not be our last resort. Be reminded that our husband's *head* is Jesus Christ and when we make our request known to Him, He says, "that the king's heart (person of authority—the husband's heart) is in My hands like streams of water that I can turn to the right or left" (Prov. 21:1). Therefore, when God changes a mind and rebukes a heart, it's a permanent change—keep praying.

Respectful

The scripture that makes *respect* a wife's *role* is:

> And let the wife see to it that she respects her husband.
> —EPHESIANS 5:33

> As they (husbands) observe your chaste and respectful behavior.
> —1 PETER 3:2

Respect is at the bedrock of a male's soul. It somehow defines the man. And it is only meaningful when reflected by those he holds in high regard. Being respected by those meaningful people in a man's life gives him definition. I am saying this to all women: We need to be respectful to this authority figure that God has set over our lives— our husbands. No, you don't have to applaud them, just be respectful of their responsibility of care for you and your family unit.

Now for some clarification, respectful does not mean agreeing. You can be respectful of the differences each spouse brings to the marriage. Wives need to show respect for their husband's authority in the marriage and home. We can still voice an opinion. However, he is responsible before God in the final choices he makes for his marriage and family. Showing respect toward your husband's authority keeps the lines of communication open between you and the issues on the table.

Granted, some may have an overbearing husband who *demands* submission and respect. Prayer is the solution, along with caution, as you embrace a posture of respectful behavior. There is more to come on this challenging subject.

Part III

Husband

He who finds a wife finds a good thing, and obtains favor from the Lord.

—Proverbs 18:22

Chapter 8

Rules: Cleave, Authority, Provide

CHALLENGES OF BECOMING A husband are equivalent to the challenges of becoming a man. Length of years cannot measure this achievement of manhood. When a man marries, although he is responsible for safe voyage of his marriage, is he equipped with skills to match the requirements of this position? Is he capable of succeeding in his manhood to achieve success as a husband?

This section of the book is directed totally to the husband, as tutored by God. Yes, wives will read this also and become better equipped to pray for and encourage their husbands.

The Husband Rules: cleave—authority—provider

The Husband Roles: lover—honor—protector

Cleave: The Husband's Rule

Let's begin with a few details about what is meant by "cleaving." Sometimes there is a clearer understanding of *cleave* by looking at what His Word does *not* mean.

Cleaving in marriage does *not* mean:

- Having a common goal
- Having the same opinion

- Doing everything together
- Being polite
- Buying lots of gifts
- Remembering her birthday and your wedding anniversary
- Seldom having an argument
- Taking out the trash (I couldn't resist, sorry)

Though this partial list may show respectful behavior, it does not show the oneness of intimacy that comes with a passion of "cleaving."

Insights About Cleaving

Insight #1: Oneness of intimacy only happens in the marriage when the husband cleaves.

The wife has no authority or role in this intimacy process.

> For this cause a man shall leave his father and mother and cleave to his wife; and the two shall become one flesh.
> —MATTHEW 19:5

Note: This scripture is conveying God's perfect plan for a healthy, happy marriage as stated clearly in three parts: *leave, cleave, one flesh.*

Part one: "For this cause a man shall leave his father and mother…" meaning the boy becomes a man. He leaves behind his childish ways of thinking, behaving, and depending on his parents. Therefore he should act, think, and behave as a man.

If the husband has not matured into manhood, he is not capable of validating his wife as a woman. It requires his manhood to draw her into a validation of womanhood. Here lies an early problem in most struggling marriages. The husband has not emotionally "left home" but has remained a boy with unmet needs. Consequently, the wife will feel drawn to *raise* her husband and drive him into his manhood, which never works. I know.

Part two: "and cleave to his wife," meaning that a husband should be emotionally equipped to draw his wife to himself, fanning over her a great desire to cleave with a deep, passionate attraction. And to embrace her with reassurance that she is desirable, worthy, and lovely in his sight (Songs of Solomon chapters four and seven).

Part three: "and the two shall become one flesh," meaning that one of the benefits of marriage and intercourse is to produce children after your own kind. The children are, therefore, the one flesh represented in physical characteristics—the two parents.

Insight #2: The wife is totally aware if her husband is cleaving or not.

> And she conceived again and bore him a son and said, now this time my husband will become attached to me...
> —GENESIS 29:34

Personal story: In many of my interviews with Christian wives, the subject of their sex life revealed that their husbands did not cleave to them from the first day of their marriage. And most wives assume it has everything to do with them. If we told anyone we had a dull sex life in our marriage, we would be confessing our failure as a lover. So we believed the lie and kept quiet.

Husbands, your wife can answer whether you are a cleaver or non-cleaver. Ask her in a non-accusing way, and she will tell you everything. There is a solution to this problem, and I applaud your courage to uncover this truth in your marriage.

Insight #3: Cleaving is retractable!

Once the husband cleaves, it is *not* a permanent attachment—surprised? Me too!

Jacob cleaved to Leah on their wedding night thinking she was Rachel. Jacob never cleaved again to Leah because he was in love with and had a passion for her sister Rachel. Leah saw the change in Jacob's non-cleaving intimacy once he married Rachel.

> Now the Lord saw that Leah was unloved...
> —Genesis 29:31

Personal story: For a husband to be able to cleave to his wife at *his* choosing came as a big surprise to me. I believed the definition that stated "to cleave," meant an attachment *forever.* I was wrong.

My late husband, Michael, in later years was not proud of the fact that he displayed an angry temper toward me the first four years of our marriage. I was so preoccupied with his temper that our lack-luster intimate life was never brought up or challenged because I had blamed myself for my lack of enthusiasm in that area.

One night during those earlier years, we were at a stand off and Michael had gone off angrily to his office in another room. Wanting peace at any cost, I went to him in a posture of a weak, soft-spoken little girl, and I admitted to being wrong just to quiet his temper and bring calm. Then I heard myself say in this quiet and sheepish voice, "Let's be intimate." I froze inside. Intimacy was always a struggle. Michael led me into our bedroom. In bed, the moment Michael touched my arm, my body responded with a great passion. One I never experienced before or after. I was stunned and confused.

The next day, when I asked what he thought of our evening of intimacy, Michael only said it was a good idea. Now I was more confused. I knew I would store the memory of that wonderful night for a future purpose. I often rehearsed that evening over and over in my mind, re-examining every breath and every movement in hopes of finding the answer as to what opened Michael's heart to draw me in and wrap me in such great passion. What was even more baffling to me, were all the attempts at passionate intimacy after that. I was back knocking on the door of his heart to let me in.

That was the only time Michael opened his heart and cleaved with a passionate desire. God revealed the answer sixteen years later, why I had that wonderful night of love and passion with my husband Michael. The mystery is solved and I plan to share this treasure with you—a little later on.

Insight #4: Cleaving means "passion" in the marriage

> Under three things the earth quakes, and under four, it cannot bear up: Under an unloved woman when she gets a husband...
>
> —Proverbs 30:21, 23

Meaning, a married woman expects to feel loved passionately by her husband with a confidence that she is the only one he desires. Otherwise the marriage will become emotionally "shaky" due to the wife's sense of rejection by her husband, a belief that he has defiled her sense of feeling cherished and desirable. What a lonely place to be in a marriage for both.

Passion is a hot word that says it all. We are all at some point, looking for our passion, whether it's in our career choice, our calling, or our marriage. Our passion brings with it, a peace and a sense of oneness to our lives, which draws us beyond ourselves, as if in a wondrous adventure orchestrated by God. When we have passion in what we lay our hands to, time stands still and everything is sweet. Passion is needed to achieve the impossible and expand our concept of living life, which is set before us for this appointed time in history. How wonderful is the rush of passion?

Webster's Dictionary defines passion as: a strong feeling; the emotions as distinguished from reason; an object of affection or enthusiasm; sexual desire.

My definition of passion is an effortless heart emotion that draws you to a person, a goal, or purpose.

Personal story: At this point, in sixteen years of my twenty-year marriage, I was totally focused on Michael's declining health and what came next. We were once again in the emergency room for his stomach tubing to be replaced. As Michael is in his wheelchair, I am waiting as I pace at the door looking for the doctor who will check Michael out and replace the tubing. I seemed to be the only one with this sense of urgency—after all this is ER—but I was also mindful that Michael's need was not a high alert.

An off-duty doctor stopped to visit with Michael. In the course of their conversation, Michael told the doctor about the book I was writing. Michael always loved the sobering look men got when I started my conversation with, "God holds the husband 100 percent accountable for the success or failure of the marriage." This often yielded a very shocked response, as I continued to share other important points in a happy marriage.

In the midst of my conversation, Michael turned and directed this statement to the doctor and said something he had never said to me or in front of me. "I love my wife dearly, but I don't have a passion for her."

I felt shocked and hurt. I couldn't even swallow my saliva let alone reply. Yet I was relieved by the calm peace that quickly enveloped me. I finally got the answer I had been looking for in my marriage to a precious man who was unable to cleave to me. He didn't have the "passion" to open his heart and draw me in—this was it in a nutshell! Although I was very upset at this revelation, I was grateful to God that He had given me part of the answer I was seeking for the lack of intimacy in my marriage. And with this revelation knowledge, came the rest of the pieces of why Michael didn't have a passion for me. It had nothing directly to do with me—to my surprise.

As noted in the story of Jacob and Leah-Genesis 29:21-35, he acted lovingly and kind towards Leah; but his passion was for Rachel, her sister. How would the story read for Jacob if he didn't have his Rachel but had to live his entire life with Leah, a woman he did not passionately love? Is this your marriage? Did you marry a woman for whom you lacked a passionate love and desire?

The moment you married, you became responsible for the success or failure of your marriage—before God. He can help you redefine your passion and reshape what is desirable to you, to create an authentic passion for your bride.

Lets recap the points made on cleaving:

- Intimate oneness *only* happens in the marriage when the husband cleaves.
- The wife is aware if her husband is cleaving or not.
- Cleaving is retractable.
- Cleaving is the "passion" in the marriage.

How does this lack of passion happen to so many husbands? Why do they not want to give themselves passionately to their wives? The answer is "Mom," was the direct statement I heard from God.

Shocked? I was. I asked God, "How is Mom the problem when you hold the man 100 percent accountable for the success or failure of the marriage?" His answer: "It's what Dad did or didn't do to Mom." A lack of intimacy could cause Mom to turn to her son and put her "emotional-straw" into his life to gain the validation she never got from her husband. It's a vicious cycle.

Most mothers would never consciously do anything wrong. However, fathers can feel relieved and less burdened when their children meet Mom's need for validation and intimacy. The only one who knows the full emotional impact of this burden to "validate Mom" is the son. And therein lies the root of a future problem for the son as he attempts to cleave and be intimate with another woman—his wife. This struggle has to do with what was done to the boy as he was growing up with Mom.

Before we venture further, I want to go on record and say to the mothers, "I understand your pain, Mom." Drawing this validation out of your son is an easier fix to your emotional well-being in your non-validated marriage than fighting with your husband and trying to explain the unexplainable. It's hard to know the name of the real enemy in your non-passionate marriage, which unfortunately, leaves you hopeless to define your needs. The answer you are looking for is to evaluate how your mother-in-law influenced your husband's sense of fear toward women.

But husbands have choices: You can accuse your mother of her past control and manipulation, you can take comfort in tracking how many generations back this has taken place, or you can say, "This will stop in *my* generation." The man is responsible before God to take his God-given authority to stop this action and reaction in his marriage. It also will give his sons clear voyage into manhood.

The emotional dynamics in a family often reveal how Mom can cause the boy at a very young age to make a profound oath or vow that will change his intimate life with his future wife forever—until denounced and destroyed. It is impossible for us to "un-ring" the bell. Only Jesus, as our advocate to the Father, can destroy the power of those spoken vows.

This is a partial list of mom's actions that could cause the boy to scream into his heart that hateful vow—"I will never be hurt like this again." His heart is hearing, "No woman will ever hurt me," this vow will establish in the boy's heart the lie that he will later believe as a truth about women—that all women will hurt him. Therefore, the boy vows protection, "I will keep my heart closed to women, and then I won't get hurt."

Here is a list of the most popular complains that men shared with me about Mom:

Mom's Actions

- Controlling
- Judgmental
- Critical
- Rejecting
- Shaming
- Blaming
- Verbal abuse
- Physical abuse
- Hard to please
- Unkind, insensitive
- Not loving or nurturing
- Absent emotionally/or physically
- Uncaring
- Overprotective (not trusting the son's choices or judgment)
- Self-focused
- And one emotional abuse that is often over looked—watching how critical Mom is toward Dad will quite likely set fear in the boy's heart toward a woman.

Well, you say, "who can escape having a mother who would not fit this list to some degree?" Mom is not God—therefore, it is not what mom has done to you—it's how you diligently attack those lies about women that are in *your* heart. Put there by you and can only be destroyed by you.

You don't have to wait for your mother's apology or confession of guilt. You and God can do business, and you can still honor your mother who gave birth to you. By the way, honor does not mean you have to agree with your mother, it just means you respect her position in your life. I honored that policeman's position in my life when he was writing out that traffic ticket. I may not agree with him, but I showed him honor as he exercised his authority.

Once this vow is spoken in anger as a direct command to the heart, "No woman will ever hurt me," the heart tabulates the information and files it for its future need. The subconscious has no rational of right or wrong. It just carries out an order, whether appropriate or inappropriate. So this vow, once spoken, often in anger and as a command, is stored by the subconscious as truth and awaits orders to move out and destroy the enemy that would hurt the host. The enemy is any woman who "smells" like mom. The power of this vow is that it switches on right after the marriage ceremony. Because the husband judged and vowed against his mother who was married and a wife herself. This vow will activate once the man marries (and deactivate if he should divorce). This is why premarital sex is not a guarantee of future sexual happiness.

Theophostic ministry states that all our stored past memories, good or bad, can be accessed with only a very small stimulus to any one of our five senses. So if the wife, in any way, acts like mom—the wife will "smell" like mom to the husband's senses and, consequently, the shutdown is quick and automatic in the heart of the husband.

I finally have an understanding of what happened to me that one fateful night when my precious Michael cleaved to me. I didn't "smell like mom"—with my soft, sheepish, child-like demeanor. I was not a threat. In all fairness, my mother-in-law has been kind and considerate to me, but left me the task of redefining truth to Michael and quieting his subconscious fears that my enthusiasm would somehow not be mistaken for his mom's aggression and control.

Uncovering this fact, this truth, this knowledge about your emotional positioning with mom is only part of the process to freedom. Below is a checklist to chart where you are now and where you want to be in your marriage. Husbands, you are the only ones who can make this change in your heart and influence the needed changes in your marriage.

Checklist to Intimate Freedom with Your Wife

1. Acknowledge to yourself and to your wife that you are not cleaving (you may have to ask her if you cleave) and that you understand it is totally your responsibility to correct this lack of intimacy in the marriage.

2. Evaluate your emotional issues with mom growing up.

3. List the negative characteristics of mom that set fear and hurt in your heart.

4. Forgive your mother, from your heart, for all the
    things she did and/or said that caused you emotional
    harm, even in the name of love.

    In all probability you will be working on number
    four for some time. If your cry for forgiveness
    toward mom doesn't make it to your heart, or
    if the heart doesn't hear a passionate cry for
    forgiveness, your heart will remain closed. In the
    heat of "your passion of hurt" you gave that direct
    order (vow) to your heart that "No one will ever
    hurt me like this again." It is with the same force of
    passion that you need to forgive your mother and
    look past her mistakes and try to understand her
    pain, her loneliness, her hurt and truly forgive her
    as you daily expect this same forgiveness from your
    heavenly Father.

    This is the hardest part of your journey to
    freedom—forgiving mom. Detailing to mom all
    the things she did to hurt you will not bring the
    freedom you are looking to achieve. In most cases,
    mom will deny the picture that you are painting
    of her behavior. I have discovered that abusive
    people do not believe they are abusive. No amount
    of conversation will change the attitude of their
    hearts. God is your way to freedom. Every time
    you hold a grudge against your mom and can not
    forgive, you "light another candle" as a symbol of
    her control over your life. Cut yourself free from

holding back forgiveness and go on with God. He has plans for your future that far exceed your imaginations (Jer. 29:11).

5. Renounce the vow (prayer listed below).

6. Forgive your father for rejecting your mother emotionally/intimately.

7. Be accountable to your wife on how well you are doing cleaving with passion (please let her be honest without regret—this will benefit both of you).

8. Be honest with yourself and recognize that you are worth loving.

The prayer below was composed as an emotional link to your heart in an effort to bring a glass of water to an angry heart. It is written that, "as water reflects the face, so the heart reflects the man" (Prov. 27:19). I have heard it said often by different Christian counselors that, "we will love the way we were loved" and to some of you that can be a frightening thought. Perhaps you blame your mother for not being aware of her shortcomings in nurturing you and meeting your emotional needs. Could this also be a similar reflection in your own marriage?

Husbands, be mindful of this spiritual law, (1 Cor. 11:7) that the woman is the glory of her husband—meaning she will reflect his attitude back to him. It is as if your wife is holding a mirror in front of her face, and you see your reflection in her. Thus you will always know how well you are doing in your marriage. Though wives are not perfect and have their own issues and problems, we are talking about the "boss," you! You have the authority to change your marriage and your family. You're the boss and the buck stops with you.

An attempt to *will* your marriage towards passionate intimacy won't disarm the directive (vow) etched into the heart of the boy. The advantage to being a born again Christian believer is that you have access to the throne of God through Jesus Christ who intercedes before the Father on your behalf. Therefore, being mindful of the power of His life-giving Word (Bible), you can make your bold declarations to Christ for his intercession to the Father to deliver you from the declaration of your words (vow). The Word of God and His knowledge on how to use it wisely is the only offensive weapon you possess.

The Husband's Prayer to Forgive Mom

My most gracious heavenly Father God, I recognize and honor you as my God and I am so grateful that Your Son, the Lord Jesus Christ, laid down his royal robe to be born in a manger only to be later crucified for my sins on the Cross. I have asked the Lord Jesus Christ into my broken life to be my Lord and Savior and my advocate to the Father. Thank you Lord Jesus for the gift of the Holy Spirit as a deposit of this great salvation.

Most holy Father in the name of Jesus Christ, I ask that you forgive me for judging my mother's hurtful actions, words and attitude toward me. Her unkindness toward me caused me to declare a "vow" to my heart, "that no woman will ever hurt me" and with that judgment, I gave a direct-command vow to my heart to close off to any woman/wife that "smells" like mom.

To Break the Vow

As an act of my will and the desire of my heart, I forgive you, mother/mom for all your hurtful words_____(list them) spoken over me.

(Lazy, stupid, loser, etc.)

I forgive you for all your hurtful actions toward me_____ (list them)

(Controlling, critical, shaming, unloving, ignoring, etc.)

I forgive you, mother/mom for being careless in how you loved me. I forgive you, mother/mom for not even being aware of the pain and hurt that you put upon my life growing up.

I forgive you, mother/mom for making me feel _____(list them)

(Inadequate, a burden, unlovable, a nothing, rejected, etc.)

In the name of Jesus, I renounce this vow I made that "No woman will ever hurt me," and the command I gave to my heart to shut down with anyone who "smells" like my mom in any way. I am no longer in agreement with this vow I made "that no woman will ever hurt me," and I declare this vow I made destroyed, disarmed, powerless, and without authority to operate in my emotions, my five senses, or my heart. And I command my heart to forget that hateful order to shut down with any woman that reminds me of my mother.

Father God, in the name of Jesus, I ask that You would wash my heart anew in the blood of Jesus and create in me a new heart and take my heart of stone and give me a new heart of flesh. And I ask You, most gracious and Holy Father God, in Your loving kindness and mercy toward me to release my heart from this vow I made to protect myself from women that "smell like mom." And I am mindful to give You, Father God, glory, honor and praise for this mighty deliverance.

To Break the Judgment

I fall out of agreement with the judgment I made "that women that look like or act like my mother will hurt me and cause me emotional pain." I nail *all* the many times I made that judgment to the "Cross of Calvary" and render the consequences of that judgment void and without authority to operate in my heart, emotions, and feelings from this day forth, in Jesus' name.

To Forgive Self

I forgive myself for the hatred I hold in my heart toward my mother for causing me to believe the "lie" that I was never good enough to love. And because this "lie" defiles the character of what God made me to be, I fall out of agreement with this "lie." And Father God, I ask in Jesus' name for You to restore my heart to love again, so that I can better love myself and reflect Your image.

Forgiveness for Mom

Gracious Father God, I ask in the name of Jesus that you would forgive my mother/mom for all the hurtful things she did and said to me growing up. I ask that you would redeem my mother from any consequences due to her harmful behavior towards me and that you would restore peace and love to my mother's heart. Amen.

These prayers will not meet your need of deliverance with quick read through. There may be parts of this prayer that your heart won't let you say at this time. Only in honesty is their deliverance. Remember the story when Jesus asked the blind man what he needed. Jesus is saying, "Have you taken an honest evaluation of your life and do you know what you are really asking of Me?" When you are speaking out His name in these prayers, be clear and honest about what you are asking. Each time you read through these prayers, take your time and make them your own. Your heart will always betray you if you refuse to listen to its pain.

Read these prayers as the five-, six-, or seven-year-old heart of a young boy. Screaming, yelling, and crying are allowed. Just say these prayers over and over until they become the truth that will defeat the lies and render powerless all its tentacles that have strangled your marriage relationship, your intimacy, and your ability to love passionately and that includes yourself.

You need to be wise on how the cycle of judgment works. It says in Romans 2:1, "Therefore you are without excuse, every man of you who passes judgment, for in that you judge another, you condemn yourself; for you who judge practice the same thing."

In other words, as you judge another person, that judgment will come back on you. As you judged the actions and attitude of your mother, it can return back to you through the actions and attitude of your wife. Now, she will really "smell like mom."

Prayer for Judgment on Wife

Gracious Holy Father God, I ask that you would deliver my wife_____, from the consequences of my judgment of my mother's hurtful actions and words. Restore my wife to her own person-hood and destroy any defilement of her personality I have caused because of this judgment towards my mother. I ask for a divine covering over my wife and a Ring of

Fire for her protection from the sowing and reaping consequences of my words, in Jesus name. Amen.

Father God; forgive me for all the many times I accused my wife _____, of acting and sounding like my mother. I ask that you would destroy those words of judgment that I spoke over my wife. That those words of judgment would have no more power or authority to defile my wife's behavior, in Jesus' name I ask this. Amen.

There will be times when your wife is talking to you and those old hateful feelings you held against your mom will creep over your heart and dash that friendly communication to the ground. Being angry with your wife because she has that God-given gift of putting her finger on unfinished work in your heart will not bring the deliverance and intimacy you desire. When this happens you need to say to your wife, thank you, turn around and say out loud and with passion the "I forgive you Mom prayer" (you may already have it memorized). Your judgment and your vow was said in anger, so when your wife makes you feel that anger again, yell out that prayer of forgiveness for mom, *at the moment* you feel this anger. Quite likely your heart will believe you this time.

This is a reprogramming for the heart to trust your wife and her feelings for you—then to trust yourself to embrace her in passionate intimacy. You may not have been loved passionately growing up, so waving this trophy of intimacy and love at the finish line may not be motivation enough to desire changing your safe place for the unknown. Once you have been passionately and intimately loved you will never want to lose that feeling or that person.

Sometimes the judgment comes in the form of judging how "Mom treated Dad." Perhaps your mother was thoughtful, kind and loving towards you, but was unkind, irritated, and insensitive to Dad in your presence. Most likely, Dad was not cleaving to Mom and she was lonely and irritated by his indifference. Had Dad loved and respected his wife, as he should, she'd be purring like a kitten! If you said to yourself—"I'll never let anyone hurt me like my mother hurt my father"—you have commanded your heart to close off for protection's sake when you marry.

Prayer for Judging Mother's Critical Behavior Toward Dad

> *Father God, forgive me for all the many times I judged my mother's critical behavior toward my Dad. Forgive me for all the many times I made the vow that I will never let my wife hurt me like my mother hurt my father. Forgive me for closing off my heart to my wife and causing her pain and loneliness because of this vow, in Jesus name. Amen.*
>
> *Mother, I forgive you for all the criticism and hurt that filled our home causing me to fear women. Dad, I forgive you for not meeting Mom's needs with oneness and passion, which caused her to be bitter and lonely in Jesus' name. Amen.*

Father God, I ask in Jesus name to destroy, disarm and render inoperative the vow and command I made to my heart to close off intimacy to women to avoid emotional pain. Amen.

As an act of my will, I fall out of agreement with the vow I made that no woman would ever get close enough to hurt me. I break my agreement forever with this judgment and render this vow without any authority to operate in my life, relationships, and marriage, in Jesus name. Amen.

If this was your situation growing up, the travel time from your head to your heart may take some time to revisit the pain and be truly sorrowful for this judgment. This is not saying your mother's actions have merit. It is saying, "Who am I to judge another person's actions?" Only God is the final judge before whom we will stand and give an account.

> For God will bring every act to judgment, everything which is hidden, whether it is good or evil.
> —ECCLESIASTES 12:14

Authority—The Husband's Rule

There can only be one boss. Everything around the boss becomes a reflection of his authority. Our Lord Jesus Christ spoke of it often in the Gospels. He would say, "I only say or do what I see the Father say or do." Jesus Christ came to reflect the Father in all that He did.

Father God is the Head Boss and our Lord Jesus knew this. So who did Father God appoint as the *Head Boss* in marriages?

God has appointed the husband as the boss over his marriage. This is not a figurehead position of responsibility without authority. God has given the husband not only the responsibility for the well-being of the marriage, but also the authority to change anything in the marriage that does not measure up to His standards.

God has given us story after story to reflect this authority of the husband over his wife and family. And to further make His point, He has revealed some of the great advantages to this authority.

First, we need to clarify who is boss. Every boss has a boss. As a husband, your boss is God Himself, in the person of the Lord Jesus Christ. The wife's boss is the husband. So the lineup of the "bosses" would look like this—God—Jesus Christ—husband—wife. This is the same picture of headship that we see in 1 Corinthians 11:3:

> I want you to understand that Christ is the head of every man, and man is the head of a woman, and God is the head of Christ.

With this headship of bosses comes order and unity. Only the boss has the authority to get the job done. So to bring the picture into sharper focus, if order and unity are missing in a marriage, the boss who is responsible is the husband. The husband is the only one that has the God-given authority to shape his marriage into order. So I might add here—as the husband goes so goes the marriage. Remember, my sweet husbands, God has given you the ability and gifting to be the boss.

Earlier in the book I discussed your authority and that your authority over your wife dates back to the Garden of Eden. This anointing of authority was given to you at birth as it was with Adam. It is irrevocable. I will explain how this mystery power works and how if misused, it can cause almost irreversible consequences.

There is an Old Testament story that makes the point of a husband's authority more respected and understandable. The story of Jacob's secret departure from his father-in-law, Laban, tells when Jacob took his two wives, children, servants, and animals and headed back to his homeland, as directed by God. (See Genesis 31:22–35 and Genesis 35:16–19.)

Unbeknownst to Jacob, his beloved Rachel, his favorite wife, had taken her father Laban's family idols and hidden them in her tent. When Laban finally caught up with Jacob and inquired of his sudden departure, he went on to say, "Why did you steal my gods?"

Jacob in exercising his authority said, "The one with whom you find your gods shall not live." Laban searched all the tents and upon entering Rachel's tent, Rachel was sitting on the family idols and asked her father to forgive her for the fact she could not rise from her seated position because she was in her womanhood (monthly cycle). Laban was unable to do a total search of Rachel's tent. Thus, Laban was unable to find his beloved family gods. Unfortunately, the death sentence was already spoken over Rachel by the only person who had the final authority over her life—Jacob, her husband.

Rachel thought she had tricked her father and fooled Jacob. This verbal death sentence was a time bomb waiting for its time to be fulfilled. As we read later on in the story, in Genesis 35:16-19, we hear of Rachel's severe labor pains, as she is giving-birth to Benjamin.

Rachel dies giving birth to Benjamin—Jacob's death sentence was now carried out. Also, Rachel died in the area she lied about in her womanhood—giving birth. Jacob did not realize when he spoke the "directive of death," that he had sentenced his beloved Rachel. That's how the voice of authority works. Ignorance of this authority does not void its fulfillment.

The death sentence Jacob made would not have been carried out had Rachel been innocent. In today's marriages, a husband has the same authority to curse his wife's life, especially when there is just cause for the curse to become effective, as in the case of Rachel's stealing and lying.

It is written, "A curse without cause does not alight" (Prov. 26:2). Meaning, if you curse your wife with a negative statement and she is not that negative statement, the curse will not take affect. But, on the other hand, if the husband repetitively speaks the same negative statement over his wife, then once the wife agrees consciously or subconsciously, ("it must be true, he tells me this all the time") with his negative statement—the curse will take affect. The husband's misuse of his authority defiled his wife and with her agreement to his spoken curse, it is established.

> Again I say to you, that if two of you agree on earth about anything that they may ask, it shall be done for them by My Father who is in heaven.
> —MATTHEW 18:19

What happens with the authority of the husband's mouth can be subtle but carries with it the same outcome. If the wife is overweight and the husband says, "You'll always be overweight because you don't control your eating habits," guess who will stay fat! Or, "Your handwriting is so poor, who can read anything that you write?" That was mine. I struggled with that for years even though my penmanship was lovely. It turned unreadable because my husband would consistently put me down in this area when irritated. He would attack my penmanship when doing *his* paperwork. Later, with divine knowledge and much remorse, he was able to apologize to me and to legally void that defiling statement off my life.

God has armed husbands with a powerful gift. This authority is to keep you and your family safe and free from harm. You are the boss and have the last word. Therefore, you will be held accountable to Him as to how well you have used this gift. Let the harvest of your mouth bring forth good fruit.

> A man will be satisfied with good by the fruit of His Words,
> and the deeds of a man's hands will return to him.
> —PROVERBS 12:14

The power of life and death is in the tongue and those of us that are tamed by it know its power. This is a wise man that understands all his spiritual gifts from God and how to use them as a blessing. Proverbs 12:18, "There is one who speaks rashly like the thrust of a sword, but the tongue of the wise brings healing." If the husband slaughters his wife with his words, he will live in the chaos he created with his mouth. The wife will mirror her husband's bad behavior back to him, and he, most likely will become offended at her unkind behavior. Thus the cycle of misunderstood authority will keep repeating and keep spouses offended.

The wife is the glory of the husband (1 Cor. 11:7), reflecting the husband's behavior back to him. The husband, therefore, is without excuse before God. He can't say, " I didn't know I acted insensitively toward my wife." All a husband has to do is listen to how his wife speaks to him. When Christian women use harsh statements, experience tells me that the husband has most often misused his authority and sown that behavior into her.

A wise husband will listen to how his wife speaks to him. If she speaks in an unkind, easily irritated manner, shock her by saying, "Honey, I am so sorry for all the times I have spoken to you in such an unkind way. Will you forgive me?" You will get her attention and her heart. You have now become the boss of authority all wives desire to follow. I realize you may have to take baby-steps at first, but you will not be disappointed with the results.

There are some great advantages of your authority over your wife. Numbers 30 says it all. Please read the entire chapter. It clearly states that the husband can annul any negative statement the wife makes with her mouth so that it will not come to pass in her life. Even the negative statements that her father failed to annul, the husband can annul. That's wonderful for the wife. How does this work?

Also observe that Numbers 30 is talking about daughters and wives. The husband cannot annul the vows or oaths that his son has bound to himself. This means the son needs to watch dad in action, so that he will be mindful that what he confesses with his mouth will carry with it future consequence or obligation. This provides a wonderful spiritual habit for his future marriage.

Understanding your positioning as the authority of your wife and family is fundamental. Most couples never understand the spiritual dynamics Father God gave when He set this irrevocable anointing upon all males. From the beginning of time, God set everything in an order that each part would function to the blessing and benefit of the other parts. He left nothing to chance except the free will of His greatest creation—His people.

But God was not caught off-guard. Knowing that our stubborn will would be our downfall, Father God had already placed His life rafts of deliverance sprinkled throughout His Word. His Word is a pearl of great value. So, as we search His Word for these truths, find them, acknowledge them, and implement them, we begin to untangle ourselves from the lies that destroy our families and ourselves.

Husbands, here is an example of how Numbers 30 can work in your marriage. Example: your wife makes a statement/vow to you that she will always be fat. That she has been fat all her life. Or perhaps, her statement/vow is tastier. Example: your wife makes a statement that she will always be a lousy cook or that she was told that she would never cook anything worth eating. At the time you first heard this statement from your wife, you would denounce this statement (vow) she made with her mouth by saying this prayer in her presence.

> *"Father God, it is written in Numbers 30 that I have the authority as a husband to annul this statement (vow) my wife_____(wife's name) made saying _____ (verbalize the statement she made) and I render this statement void and inoperative in her life. This statement _____ has no further authority to operate in my wife's life, health,*

or relationships. I ask in Jesus' name that _____
(wife's name) be restored to wholeness emotionally,
spiritually, and physically in all areas. Amen."

You probably have a good idea of the issues your wife struggles to overcome. Some of the negative vows/oaths she says with her mouth most likely came from her growing up years and other vows/oaths are perhaps your handiwork in her life. Either way, you have the authority to void these negative spoken confessions/vows she makes.

It would also be wise that once you have annulled her negative statement/vow to then speak a positive statement of fact in its place. Example, "Yes, you are a good cook. You are very teachable, I admire your ability to learn new creative cooking techniques."

How beautiful is this gifting from God? When I shared the revelation of Numbers 30 with my late husband, he was delighted to annul anything and everything I vowed and everything he had confessed over me. He was able to void that statement he made that I had poor penmanship, and watched as my penmanship was restored to its former glory.

As I remembered statements that my precious father (perhaps carelessly) spoke over me, that had defiled me in some way, I would come running to Michael and say, "Numbers 30" and he knew to listen up because he was about to set me free of another lie. How wonderful was this? Freedom was becoming my constant companion.

Husbands, if your father misused his authority over your mother, you, and your siblings, forgive Dad. It's not worth the consequences you will reap in feeling qualified to judge your father's behavior.

Meaning, when you marry you will reflect your father's behavior in your marriage. If you don't like how Dad treated Mom, then start forgiving Dad, because he was probably acting like his own father. Check it out. As you glance up the generational line of father to son— you will see repeated similarities in behavior.

Now we see a glimpse of how sin can travel down a family line. Fortunately, the Cross of Calvary is always available to the Christian husband struggling with negative habits and traits transmitted to him by the sins of his father. And who also desires to stop it with his generation. Wouldn't that be a wonderful gift to give your son—a gift that would definitely keep giving?

> A righteous man who walks in his integrity, how blessed are his sons after him.
>
> —PROVERBS 20:7

Husband's Prayer

Father God I ask in Jesus name, that You would forgive me for all the many times and for all the many ways I judged my father's behavior as a father and as a husband. And I ask that you would deliver me from the consequences of these judgments in my life and in my marriage. Create in me a pure heart and renew a right spirit in me. Amen.

"Let the words of my mouth and the meditation of my heart be acceptable in Thy sight, O Lord, my rock and my Redeemer."
—PSALMS 19:14

This prayer, spoken daily, makes an excellent point in fine-tuning your communication skills of authority. God wants to help. His Word is powerful and it will never return to you void. It is also a true way to be accountable to your boss, Jesus Christ.

In closing, be aware husbands, your spoken verbal authority is given to you until you die. Which means, that at any time, you can continue to speak blessings and/or curses over your wife and over your sons and daughters, even after they marry.

This same authority holds true for your father and father-in-law, who can bless or curse your life. They can use the authority of their spoken words to criticize, rebuke, and judge over your life and marriage, though they may not be mindful of this authority. Laban, Jacob's father-in-law, is speaking to Jacob in Genesis 31:29, "It is in *my* power to do you harm, but the God of your father spoke to me last night, saying, 'Be careful not to speak either good or bad to Jacob.'"

Husbands should keep a short account on all negative issues and unresolved conflicts with parents and in-laws. When they speak over you, your wife, and your family, it should be with words of blessing. Forgive where necessary, in your heart and with your words. Honoring your parents and in-laws is not debatable. It doesn't mean you agree with their behavior. It just means you can state your opinion in an honoring manner because of their positioning over your life. It also wouldn't be a bad idea to keep Numbers 30 handy—just in case.

There is much harmony in a marriage when the husband handles rightfully the Word of God with his actions and with his words.

"He who gives attention to the word shall find good, and blessed is he who trusts in the Lord."

—Proverbs 16:20

May your blanket of authority over your wife bring to her a feeling of being cherished, nurtured, and safe. In like matter, may her reflection of your love warm your heart.

Provider—The Husband's Rule

"Challenged" is the feeling I often get when talking with husbands about providing for their family's financial needs and in some cases—wants. This was the same with my late husband. During our twenty-year marriage, I became an avid reader on the spiritual cause and effects of financial struggles in Christian marriages. After all, a Christian lifestyle guarantees the shortest trip to the "pot of gold" right? Wrong! This road trip to the pot of gold is to some, a race against time, to have more money than days at the end of each month. Why and how does this happen?

Let's examine some truths and untruths about the husband and wife's role in providing income for the family unit. We clearly understand from God's Word that the husband is the designated provider of the total income for his family. This fact is supported in the following scriptures.

In Genesis 3:16, God is stating to Eve in the presence of Adam, "and he (Adam) shall rule over you."

What God is saying to Eve is that He has put Adam in charge of her welfare (to rule). Feeding her, keeping her safe, clothing her, protecting her, providing shelter for her was given to Adam as his responsibility. As was the garden God gave Adam to rule.

Perhaps you have heard it preached that this scripture meant that the wife was to bow to the husband's rule over her life. This is stretching God's point. There is no doubt that God made the husband the head over the wife, and with that, the responsibility to provide for her.

Because of Eve's disobedience to Adam's order from God not to eat from the tree in the middle of the garden, God made Adam responsible for Eve's decisions and any consequences that followed. In Genesis 3:17, Then to Adam God said, "Because you have listened to the voice of your wife, and have eaten from the tree about which I commanded you, saying, "You shall not eat from it." Cursed is the ground because of you. In toil you shall eat of it all the days of your life." This line of "responsibility as the provider" is the husband's and it flows down to all husbands today from their great-grandfather, Adam. Still, you will find that pot of gold, because in Proverbs it is written, "that wisdom is better than gold and understanding better than silver."

Who desires more wisdom? We will use God's Word to underscore each point. If the husband is incapable or hindered from providing adequate income to cover the total financial needs for his wife and family, there are other factors to consider.

Some Hindering Factors

Factor #1: Living beyond your means—with a house too large, too expensive, poor control of credit charge usage, buying on impulse, and other careless habits.

Factor #2: You have struggled all your life with making money and handling finances.

Factor #3: You believe your wife should help with providing some of the income, after all, she adds to the bills and financial needs.

Factor #4: You lack knowledge of God's laws for abundant living.

Factor #1: Living beyond your means.

This should be an easy fix. Reevaluate with your wife what you can and cannot afford and make the appropriate changes. If it means downsizing to a smaller home or owning only one car, you are the head, the boss. You call the family meeting, you come up with a game plan, and you follow through on decisions that are made. Remember the wife is the "helper," not the leader or the initiator. You are.

Let's get sober on this responsibility. Revamp your asset pool and seek professional help if necessary. Look into Christian counseling on finances (Crown Ministries) or seek a qualified Christian counselor who can help with struggles in manhood issues in "leaving father and mother."

In all labor there is profit, but mere talks leads only to poverty.
—PROVERBS 14:23

The late Larry Burkett of Christian Financial Concepts devoted his adult life and his ministry to teaching on Christian financial responsibilities. With a sense of humor as only he could deliver, Larry had wisdom in his techniques to uncover the "why" a family struggled financial. Larry said, "When meeting with a husband with money problems, I insist that his wife be present. She will tell me everything I need to know as to why he is in debt."[1] I have seen this truth played out in other marriages that struggle in this area. So men, be wise, the answer to your financial problems could be lying next to you in bed—ask her.

Perhaps your wife's over-spending is the reason for your debt. You are still the boss, and you need to exercise authority and limit her spending. Settling this issue may take some time, but it is vitally important. Also, check out the "mirror" of your reflection. Could her need to overspend be your reflection of rebellion? Give communication a chance to reveal the real enemy in this financial dilemma. You may be surprised at the answers.

Factor #2: All my life I have struggled with making money and handling finances.

The "all my life" part of the statement, sounds like a curse and only a curse with a legal right to you can take root. Where is the open door to this legal right? In Leviticus 26:3–4, it is written, "If you walk in My statutes and keep My commandments so as to carry them out, then I shall give you rains in their season, so that the land will yield its produce and the trees of the field will bear their fruit."

The "keep My commandments so as to carry them out" points to the problem of how this legal ground is established that gives the right of way for the curse to alight. Proverbs 26:2: "So a curse without cause does not alight."

The Ten Commandments are all favorites of mine—some are easier to obey naturally, while others require more raw obedience. However, there is only one Commandment that carries with it a promise and that promise can either be the wind under your sail to financial prosperity or an anchor that keeps you financially bankrupt. It states in the fifth Commandment—Exodus 20:12—"Honor your father and mother that your days will be long (and everything will go well for you) in the land, which the Lord your God gives you." In whatever area that you dishonor your parents, it will not go well for you.

Your parents and in-laws have authority from God to bless or curse your life verbally depending on how you honor or dishonor them during their lifetime. When we step out of our rebellion and self-focused pain and obey God's commandment, we break cycles of failure.

As a son growing, if you were disobedient to your parent's wishes in handling money or didn't honor them in seeking their advice about major financial decisions, they may have unintentionally spoken a curse of financial failure over your life. Intentionally or not the curse will still operate, if there is legal ground. Remember, honoring doesn't mean that you agree. Honoring means showing respect to your parents so that you won't be subject to their words in a negative way. You can respectfully agree to disagree. I think you know how that works.

Most parents want the best for their children, but often have little idea of the authority they exercise when speaking into their children's lives, especially as the child is growing up. Perhaps the child in his eagerness to express "choices" made an unwise decision, which is sharply corrected by a parent. This could set up rebellion in the heart of the child. When the seeds of dishonoring are sowed, the harvest time will surely come—reaping later than he sowed and more than he sowed. That's God's law of reaping. Sowing and reaping includes both good and bad seeds planted. Ignorance of God's law won't grant you favor.

Michael's Story

Michael's parents were good people. However, they were very stern and controlling. He rebelled against their control and criticism in silent disobedience. He could never seem to please his parents in any decision he made. Nothing ever seemed good enough. He gave up thinking he would ever receive a blessing from their mouths, though he held out hope that making straight A's in school and skipping two grades to graduate from high school at age sixteen might merit that blessing, still it didn't come—it wasn't enough.

His college major was in the field his parents felt suited him best. Upon graduation he was hired by a large company and worked for five years with rapid promotions. Mike began to panic because he "believed" he was not good enough and that his promotions would reveal his inability to handle new responsibilities. Fear of failure and lack of self-confidence led Michael to make a radical change in employment. Without consulting his parents, he left his secure job with all its insurance packages and retirement programs for a stock-broker's position with limited benefits.

Needless to say, both parents were outraged by his decision. The words that followed, "you are so stupid, you just left the best job you will ever have. Where was your brain when you decided to leave that secure job with all those future benefits?" As Michael gave validity to their statements, their curse was established. This became the anchor to Michael's financial struggles his entire adult life. Despite a lot of hard work and very creative ventures, this curse stole victory, every time, from Michael's efforts to succeed.

> Train up a child in the way he should go, even when he is old he will not depart from it.
> —PROVERBS 22:6

"The way you train up a child *is* the way he will go and even when he is old he will not depart from it" would be the more realistic translation of this scripture. Parents need to choose their words wisely in correcting their children.

> And, fathers, do not provoke your children to anger; but bring them up in the discipline and instruction of the Lord.
> —EPHESIANS 6:4

> Fathers, do not exasperate your children, that they may not lose heart.
> —COLOSSIANS 3:21

Through much counsel, Bible reading, and Holy Spirit guidance, came understanding and the revelation knowledge by which Michael began the process to disarm the curses and re-harvest seeds for blessings. Though the process was started, Michael ran out of time. Struggling with a twenty-year illness, he stepped into Glory before he could finish. His work may not have finished here, personally for himself, but the knowledge of this truth is left for you.

I would add that your financial struggle could also be connected to your wife and her rebellion with her parents growing up. If she were "cursed" by the words of her parents' disagreement in her choices of employment, etc., it would also carry the same financial challenges and losses over her life. If not dealt with, it will carry over into her partnership with you in marriage, especially if she is partnered with you in business. If this is the case for your wife, you can annul her confession when she puts into words the verbal curses her parents spoke over her life. Remember Numbers 30? She can also pray the prayers below to seal off any further attacks of the enemy.

In conclusion, we can't leave out the authority your in-laws have over your life to bless or curse. Remember Genesis 31:29—Laban, Jacob's father-in-law, had the authority to curse Jacob's life, but God prevented him from speaking good or bad over Jacob. You may wish to add your in-laws to the prayers below. Where apologies towards them are needed, do so. Being "right" does not always bring a blessing or bring about the changes for which you are hoping. Let us move on with life.

The prayer for disarming the financial curse and planting seeds for a blessing is a two-step process.

First is the prayer to forgive your parents and in-laws for the financial curses they have spoken over you.

Second is for you to fall out of agreement with the "lies" you have believed about your ability to succeed financially.

The prayers below are a guideline for your financial deliverance—choose what is suitable to your situation.

First Prayer

Most Holy Father, I forgive my parents for all their hurtful, unkind words they have spoken over my life. I forgive them for their control and criticism over the decisions I made in trying to please them. I forgive them for hurting me with their actions and reactions towards me.

Father God, forgive me for my disobedience toward my parents and for cursing them in my heart. Forgive me for all the ways I dishonored my parents with my words and my actions, I ask this in Jesus name, Amen.

Father God, I ask in Jesus name that you would forgive my parents for the many times they cursed my life with their words. Forgive me Father God, for the many times I provoked my parents, by my disobedience, to speak "financial failure" curses over my life and over my ability to earn a successful income.

As an act of my will in obedience to God and with a heart that grieves, I forgive my parents. I forgive them for all the times they told me that (fill in the blank) _____ (i.e., I'll never be successful, I'll always be a failure, that I am stupid, I make stupid decisions, they would have to support you the rest of our lives etc). I forgive my parents for their lack of confidence in me as a man to make the right decisions. I forgive my parents for the fear of failure they caused me to embrace. I forgive my parents for all the emotional and financial hardships they placed over my life by the choice and authority of their negative words, which hampered my ability to be financially successful, in Jesus' name, Amen.

Father God I ask in Jesus' name that you would show me in the way I should go, and lead me in the way to profit, that I would be the head and not the tail. That I would be the lender and not the borrower, that as I apply my heart to discipline and my ears to Your words of knowledge, that the reward of humility and respect from You would be riches, honor, and life, Amen.

Second Prayer

Father God, You say in Your Word that where two agree as touching one thing, You agree. By Your Word and by the authority of my free will, I break my agreement with all the negative words spoken by my parents over me and for all the many times my parents used those negative words to curse my life, my finances, and my ability to be successful. Therefore, I break my agreement on the many times those negative words and verbal curses were spoken over me by my parents, which I now declare, in Jesus name, are forever disarmed and rendered powerless, lacking authority to rule over my life, Amen.

Father God, I ask in Jesus name that according to Proverbs 21:1 You say, " My parent's hearts (the authority) are in Your hand as streams of water that You can turn to the right or left." I ask for Your favor that You would move on my parent's hearts and to break all their agreements they made between each other concerning all the financial curses they have spoken over my ability to make good financial decisions and to earn a substantial income. I am so ever mindful to give You the honor and praise, Amen.

Lord Jesus, I thank You for taking not only my confused sins to the Cross, but my sins that caused the verbal curses by my parents. Therefore, I put the Cross of Calvary between my parents and myself and I nail to the Cross all the negative words and verbal curses that my parents spoke over my life. And in the name of Jesus, I render those negative words and verbal curses power-less in my life and without authority to operate in any area of my life, my family and my finances, Amen.

These prayers are an outline for you to follow, personalize, and adapt for your situation. When saying these prayers, remember that unless these prayers come from the heart—which may take some time—you will see little or no change.

The Prayer

Father God, I ask in Jesus' name, that you forgive me for my rebellion and disobedience toward You because of the parents You chose for me. Forgive me for not trusting the decisions and choices You have chosen for my life. Re-center me in Your perfect will for my life and grant me wisdom and favor to fulfill my life's purpose, Amen.

Factor #3: You believe your wife should be providing some of the income, she adds to the bills and financial needs.

One of the hallmarks of manhood is how a husband trusts his wife to make the right decisions for him and the family. If you can't fully trust your wife, she will reflect this negative attitude back to you. Or, it could be that you didn't trust your mother to do the right thing by you.

Either way, the ball of not trusting women is still in your court. This attitude is one most husbands do not consciously understand and have no idea about its impact on their marriage. Your wife's reactions should make you very aware of this conflict concerning trust. Having their husband's trust is a badge of honor, and they don't take it lightly.

> The heart of her husband trusts in her.
>
> —PROVERBS 31:11

This scripture states that the husband first trusts his wife. She is not presumed unworthy, needing to earn his trust. When a wife knows that she has the unconditional trust of her husband, she will do him good and not harm all the days of her life.

Controlling your wife is not a healthy alternative to not trusting your wife to do the right thing by you. You may think the right thing is for your wife to help pay your bills. This is not God's choice. Each spouse has his own set of rules to fulfill. The husband is responsible before God to provide and care for his family. God said to Adam that he would toil by the sweat of his brow to provide for his family (Genesis 3:18–19). God hasn't changed His mind.

Your wife is your helper, and is not responsible as a breadwinner. Her help should free you to advance your career and earning capacity. However, she is powerless to "fix" it if you do not earn enough income for your family. She can be the bandage that covers your shortfall by working each month—indefinitely. The *indefinitely* hinders a sense of protection all wives need to feel secure. With the husband's need to be respected by his wife and family, the wife is left with few choices. If there are children involved, the wife believes she must go back to work to earn the needed income. The husband not only misses his blessing from God, but he misses the answer to his dilemma. But God can wait.

At times, the wife may agree to help out financially when a common goal is established, buying a home, tuition for college, a new business. However, there should be an end date established to the length of time required for the wife to work.

If a husband becomes unable to work, and the full responsibility falls to the wife to provide income, pray for her. Be very vocal in your statements of kindness and over-the-top compliments. It will pay long dividends and her feet and heart won't hurt so much. This is a hard road to travel for your wife, who has half your physical strength. There is no crash course on how to live for two people.

It would be foolish for a man to buy a house based on two incomes. The home's purchase value should be based on the husband's income alone with mortgage payments in line with what he can afford, so the home isn't lost if one loses income. This may be a new concept for some. It is a safe way to protect your home during down economic times.

Your wife may have her own passion, which she may want to continue after she is married, perhaps as a doctor, nurse, writer, or school teacher. When your wife is engaged in her "passion," it's not work.

> Give her the product of her hands, and let her works praise her in the gates.
>
> —PROVERBS 31:31

This could be a double blessing to you. Her passion keeps her the woman you married and her added income will bless you at her discretion. However, a wife who desires to stay at home but has taken a job to cover the bills her husband's income can't cover, will bring that silent disrespect men dislike so much.

Our pastor, Dr. Paul L. Walker, advised Michael in our pre-martial counseling session, "Give your wife her own allowance each month. This should be money for which she will not be accountable to you. Monies that she can spend as she pleases with no objections." He is such a wise man!

Saying to your wife, "Take out of our income what you need," is not the same thing as the free passage for her to buy those dreamy purple shoes she has had her eye on for a month. Those purple shoes are not a need but a want, and that's the reward of a monthly allowance. This monthly reward will go a long way in reflecting your interest in her contentment and sense of well-being. The amount isn't the issue. It is the monthly effort on your part—the commitment—that counts.

Inheritance

A wife's inheritance of money can challenge a husband's need to control. Most husbands probably think that what is hers, is his—wrong. Helping her to invest her money, with unsolicited advice, is counterproductive and reflects your insecurity. Husbands, most wives will do the right thing by you, relax. Now, it may not fit your time schedule and you may feel she has an upper hand, but she is more than aware of the financial needs of the family and, after all, it is her money to redirect at her discretion. Help her celebrate, and don't berate her or make her feel guilty with misquoted scriptures of oneness.

If you are anxious, God may be showing you wounded areas in your heart that steal your financial blessings. Be grateful that He cares enough to give you that "ouch" to get your attention. It could be a much deeper root than her monies and your control. He knows.

> In all the land no women were found so fair as Job's daughters;
> and their father gave them inheritance among their brothers.
> —JOB 42:15

The way you treat your wife could affect your income. You probably knew this already, or are at least suspicious of its relevancy. Let us clarify this point from God's perspective.

Reading in Malachi 2:13–14 (paraphrased) "Why do you weep and groan at My alter, don't you know I have been a witness watching how you have treated the wife of your youth."

I don't believe this husband was crying at God's altar because he was struggling in his relationship with his wife. No, I believe he is crying because most of his cows and livestock were dying. He was losing income. Now, what foolish wife would step in front of God and take the heat off her husband? Most of them—me included. I know that feeling. Most wives are convinced, controlled, threatened, or talked into believing they are acting as righteous helpers when they bring in the needed extra monies. God just crosses His arms and says, something to this effect, "I have all the time in the world, when the heat is hot enough, he will look for Me."

God can withhold income, money, or financial opportunities because of how a man treats his wife. He is very serious on this. In 1 Peter 3:7, He says your prayers for help could fall on deaf ears. Often a man's bad relationship with his wife actually robs him of financial fruitfulness.

Divorced Men

I am adding this footnote for divorced men here, while discussing Malachi 2:13–14.

Knowledge is a powerful ally. I don't want you to be ignorant of His consequences. God often uses financial losses and money problems to get a man's attention.

Malachi 2:15 says, "the wife of your youth." Meaning your *first* wife and in some cases, your first and second wives (could be more). God holds you responsible still for the emotional, physical, and spiritual well-being for the—wife of your youth. And also, for any additional wives that were not married before their marriage to you.

You are accountable to God as to how well you exercised the God-given "authority of your mouth" over her life. God does not void His immutable laws.

> The wife of your youth—is your companion and your wife by covenant—let no one deal treacherously against the wife of your youth—for I hate divorce, says the Lord, the God of Israel.
> —MALACHI 2:14–16 (AUTHOR'S PARAPHRASE)

You cannot depend on your ex-wife's second husband to neutralize your handiwork over her life. You could plan on explaining and educating him on the wisdom and use of Numbers 30. Until that time, your ex-wife is still on your "score card." So how you have treated the wife/wives of your youth, could affect the present success of those financial opportunities.

Simply contacting your ex-wife (or wives) to apologize for your past bad behavior is not enough. This is not a check-it-off-your-list project. It is important to ask God to show you your attitude and actions towards your ex-wife, and become aware of the emotional pain she felt while under your care. If there were multiple marriages, the same offences may be hurting your present wife. Ask her. She may be able to shed light on those defiling character flaws that keep repeating in your marriages.

When you have done business with God and your current wife, write that letter of apology to your ex-wife. What you sowed into your wife is what you hear out of her mouth. By this, you know how you hurt her and how you reshaped her self-image. A husband's poor care hinders a wife's ability to hear and trust God. You are the one God set apart and anointed to make your marriage a reflection of loving-kindness and intimacy towards Him. What is wrong with your picture? What is wrong with your relationship with God? He wants your attention. He's waiting. And He loves you.

Do not be disappointed if there is no thank you or acknowledgement from your ex-wife on your note of contrition, asking forgiveness. We sometimes forget the sowing and reaping principle—it is more than we sowed. So how many times do you need to apologize? How many times did you make her cry? This is why I have added to all my prayers the words "for all the many times." Because God has that count and it's accurate.

You might want to start with your current wife in asking her forgiveness and as you see success, move on to your former wife. The voiding of negative statements spoken by you over your current wife and past wife needs to be done, and you are the one accountable to God to do it (unless her second husband understands and exercises his authority of Numbers 30).

Am I a financial planner? Do I have a degree in finances? No, and no, are the answers. All I know is what the Word of God has to say about finances and the person He has designated responsible to care and provide for his family and why.

#4: You lack knowledge of God's Laws for abundant living.

It says in Hosea 4:6, "That my people are destroyed for lack of knowledge." We cannot fault God for the financial fallout from disobeying His rules, if we refuse to read up on them. For some, experience will have to be our best teacher. For others, who believe God's and their parent's wise counsel on handling money, they will reap a harvest. Remember, it is never too late with God.

Once we read the scriptures below and know what God requires in handling money, refusing to obey His instructions amounts to sin (James 4:17). This scripture applies to all of the Word of God. Be knowledgeable and examine what motivates your choices in handling money. Points listed below will sharpen your understanding of what God requires, especially for husbands as the breadwinner for their wife and family.

Pay Your Taxes (No Cheating, Please)

"Render to Caesar the things that are Caesar's; and to God the things that are God's." This was Jesus' answer when He was tested with a question on whether He and His followers should pay taxes (Matt. 22:21). Jesus gives us a clear understanding of responsibility and obligation to pay our taxes. Jesus showed us by example the righteousness of paying taxes that are due. We would be foolish to question the need of this obligation.

The apostle Paul states that the government and its rules were set down for order and compliance, and those who disobey will be punished.

> For because of this you should pay taxes, for rulers are servants of God, devoting themselves to this very thing.
> —Romans 13:6

If you have not paid your taxes in full, or lied on your taxes, or cheated the government out of their income and gotten away with it, be aware of the consequences He will allow to play out in your life. God is serious about shaping you into righteousness.

Please read what God did to Ananias and his wife Sapphira when they lied to Peter about the amount of money they got from the sale of their property. They fell to their feet and breathed their last (See Acts 5:3–10.)

If you have an issue with where and how the tax dollars are spent in your state, or even on a national level, take up your banner and become a righteous instrument to evoke change. Who knows, this could be a hidden passion that just needs some stoking.

The Sabbath Rest

God calls us to a Sabbath rest. The Fourth Commandment:

> Remember the sabbath, to keep it holy. Six days you shall labor and do all your work, but the seventh day is a sabbath of the Lord your God; in it you shall not do any work...there-fore the Lord blessed the Sabbath day and made it holy.
> —EXODUS 20:8–11

> If because of the Sabbath, you turn your foot from doing you own pleasure on My holy day, And call the Sabbath a delight, the holy day of the Lord honorable, and honor it, desisting from your own ways, from seeking your own pleasure, and speaking your own word. Then you will take delight in the Lord, and I will make you ride on the heights of the earth; and

> I will feed you with the heritage of Jacob your father, for the
> mouth of the Lord has spoken.
>
> —ISAIAH 58:13–14

Is God asking us to obey the letter of the law or the spirit of the law? I believe it's worthy to consider this as a very important issue with God, or it wouldn't be one of the Ten Commandments. It most likely reflects our need for down time with Him and a time of refreshing for our spirit.

How we do this is an open-ended choice. It could be church each Sunday with no shopping in the malls, or shopping online, or working at a job. If your job causes you to work on Sunday, then another day (the total day) during the week should be set aside for your rest with the Lord.

> So there remains a sabbath rest for the people of God. For the
> one who has entered His rest has himself also rested from his
> works, as God did from His. Therefore, let us be diligent to
> enter that rest, so that no one will fall, through following the
> same example of disobedience.
>
> —HEBREWS 4:9–11

I think you understand His message and its consequences.

In going to church, you have an opportunity for Christian fellowship and to increase your faith. "Faith comes from hearing and hearing the word of Christ" (Rom. 10:17). You must determine in your heart what best honors God in your life. You will give an account of this in the future, so decide wisely.

Thought: How did this statement—"to rest on the Sabbath," make it into the top Ten? Obedience to God does not require an answer.

> On the contrary, who are you, O man, who answers back to
> God? The thing molded will not say to the molder, "why did
> you make me like this, will it? Or does not the potter have a
> right over the clay, to make from the same lump one vessel
> for honorable use and another for common use"?
>
> —ROMANS 9:20–21

The need I have for worship in song and praise is met in my Sunday church attendance. Coupled with the sermon message, His Word "teaches" me and in some cases "rebukes" me, to obey and trust Him. As I embrace His truths, I learn what He requires of my life.

The unsaved world "watches" a Christian's behavior on Sunday. This is where we can fail God by reflecting Him so poorly, for the sake of our own conveniences. The sacrifice of praise and sacrifice of stepping away from our own agenda honors God. This issue of how best to observe your Sabbath rest is something each of you should take up with God.

Pay Your Tithe

Several scriptures teach us to tithe to God. My favorite is Malachi 3:10–11:

> Bring the whole tithe into the storehouse, so that there may
> be food in My house, and test Me now in this, says the Lord
> of hosts, "If I will not open for you the windows of heaven,
> and pour out for you a blessing until it overflows. Then I will
> rebuke the devourer for you, so that it may not destroy the

fruits of the ground; nor will your vine in the field cast its grapes," says the Lord of hosts.

We know that God does not need our money. He needs our obedience. We will be tested in this area because God knows that where our treasure is, so is our heart. God wants a heart that loves Him and loves His Laws. The love of money is the *root* of all evil. Therefore money, in itself, is not evil.

The minimum tithe is 10 percent. People often seem confused as to which part of their income should be tithed. There are three possible suggestions:

1. Tithe 10 percent on your take home pay, which is net

2. Tithe 10 percent on your gross income before deductions

3. Tithe 10 percent on your earnings after taxes and FICA are deducted

God will show you His answer. Although I personally don't think number one is a valid choice because the deductions for the net income may include savings, investment options, and health insurance. God's portion should be taken out of all disposable income.

The tithe belongs to the church that you either attend weekly or the church that churches you from home. Be wise about where you place your tithe.

Now this I say, he who sows sparingly shall also reap sparingly; and he who sows bountifully shall also reap bountifully.

And God is able to make all grace abound to you, that always having all sufficiency in everything, you may have an abundance for every good deed. Now He who supplies seed to the sower and bread for food, will supply and multiply your seed for sowing and increase the harvest of your righteousness.
—2 CORINTHIANS 9:6, 8, 10

What a wonderful promise to count on.

The "offering" is money given after we tithe. As God blesses us, we bless others. God will show you where to sow this financial seed. Thus your financial picture expands and increases.

When we tithe, we are making a covenant with God, acknowledging his ownership of all that we have and that this 10 percent of our earnings is His and His alone. What a small price to pay for that eternal reward and provision from God. This posture of His ownership keeps us humble and in a position to expect a blessing of protection over our finances because He promises, "He will rebuke the devourer for us" (Mal. 3:11). Obedience is better than sacrifice because it carries with it a just reward, which far outreaches the financial.

Martha's Story

During a luncheon with a Christian lady friend, she was almost in tears. Her husband of thirty years was between jobs, and was unemployed. She loved him deeply and was frustrated with his inability to make an adequate living for their family. Although she worked part-time when the children left home, she didn't feel led to work full-time to help with the finances. They were about to lose their home of thirty years. She was frustrated and angry. Her husband did not tithe but gave only token amounts. Martha's husband was a preacher's son, whose father was very strict and unyielding. He was told that he couldn't move in the pew, and that his focus was to be on the preacher (his father). I feel her husband rebelled against God in his heart, and that rebellion grew over the years into disrespect toward God and His tithe.

Martha decided to "watch the glass fall off the table," and the glass did fall. They lost their home and moved into a small apartment. Surely now he would see her disappointment and anguish and change his ways. No, it didn't happen. He was insolated from rebuke, until he took a Crown Ministries™ course on Christian finances.

I had lost track of Martha over the next several years. Then I saw her husband on stage at our church, giving an announcement. He spoke about upcoming courses offered by Crown Ministries and gave some personal testimony. He raised his hand in the direction Martha was seated and asked her to stand. He told the story of his rebellion toward the tithe, the emotional pain and suffering he put Martha through, the loss of their home, and the fact she obeyed God by standing by him. He said she did not enable him by paying his bills, but prayed for him without ceasing.

In studying the Crown Ministries courses, he was able to *see* God in a loving new light. He now tithes and works with Crown Ministries. He bought Martha a new home and applauded her publicly after first asking her forgiveness for his rebellion and disobedience to God. There wasn't a dry eye in the congregation.

Obey the Authorities

Every person is to be in subjection to the governing authorities For there is no authority except from God, and those which exist are established by God. Therefore whoever resists authority has opposed the ordinance of God; and they who have opposed will receive condemnation upon themselves. For rulers are not a cause of fear for good behavior, but for evil. Do you want to have no fear of authority? Do what is good, and you will have praise from the same; for it is a minister of God to you for good. But if you do what is evil, be afraid; for it does not bear the sword for nothing; for it is a minister of God, an avenger who brings wrath upon the one who practices evil.

—ROMANS 13:1–4

Rebelling against authority often represents a knee-jerk reaction to our rebellion against parental authority. Choose your prayer from the above prayers in this chapter. You know which authority issues need to be dealt with. Time is not your friend. Only dealing with your issues will make the pain stop.

Be Trustworthy with Money

If God sees that you are trustworthy with a little—He will trust you with a lot. Do not begrudge small beginnings.

Do not withhold good from those to whom it is due, when it is in your power to do it.

—PROVERBS 3:27

Poor is he who works with a negligent hand, but the hand of the diligent makes rich.

—PROVERBS 10:4

It is the blessing of the Lord that makes rich, and He adds no sorrow to it.

—PROVERBS 10:22

The wicked earns deceptive wages, but he who sows righteousness gets a true reward.

—PROVERBS 11:18

The generous man will be prosperous, and he who waters will himself be watered.

—PROVERBS 11:25

Being aware of God's presence when handling monies is our best tool for financial obedience. Developing this spiritual muscle of obedience in finances can be an ongoing workout. My own learning curve included mastering rebellion.

Joy's Story

After ten years as a successful lingerie buyer for a large Atlanta department store, I began to desire my own business. My dream became reality in 1983 when I opened my designer lingerie shop with its large assortment of premier labels in an upscale area of my city. My excitement was only equaled by the anxiety I felt with the large U.S. Small Business Administration loan and its lock on the equity of my condo for security, which covered only 20 percent of the debt.

As this debt obligation hung over my head day after day, I became more and more aware that this shop was the biggest mistake of my life. Did I really wait on God for the green light? After all, I could blame it on my spiritual immaturity as a new Christian of only two years. As a believer, who tithed the full amount, went to church three times a week and read the Word daily—surely there was a break in there someplace for me.

The nine years I had my lingerie business, I struggled to make a profit. I couldn't understand why this was happening let alone how I was to correct it. After all, I considered myself a smart merchant.

An insight:

(I did find the answer to my financial struggle in 2004, twelve years *after* the shop closed in 1992. God reminded me of my actions and decisions that had dishonored my parents' authority over my life. It started when I left my secure position at a leading department store without their blessing. I dishonored them, and they unintentionally spoke a financial curse over my life—"That I would never find a good paying job or have a business success like the job I left." They felt heartsick over my decision to leave this excellent job. Being single and ignorant of God's Word, I was clueless about the cycle on which I put my life. In 2004, the curses were revealed. I was married and we were familiar with the husband's authority according to Numbers 30. After my many prayers of forgiveness for dishonoring my parents and prayers of contrition to Father God, my husband exercised his authority and annulled and voided the curses of financial failure, spoken over me by my parents.)

In 1992, toward the end of the nine years of financial struggles with my shop, I had spiritual muscles I didn't think were possible.

Though I struggled with the business, I was consistently surprised by God's provision, which further confirmed His irrevocable promises of favor so often illustrated in His Word. In some ways, I felt undaunted by the challenges I faced daily with my business—until the real test came.

The Small Business Administration (SBA) was talking to me about liquidation and I was still holding out hope for God to come through with His promises—I felt I was doing my part as a Christian. Not knowing that this "curse" was blocking my success, I still pressed on. The Georgia power company was about to pull the plug, and I was two weeks behind in paying my two part-time employees. This had never happened before. I was frustrated and confused.

On a wet, rainy day, with no customers in the shop, a man came in with the goal of buying a silk robe for his wife's anniversary gift. To quote him, "Because I have not been treating her the way a Christian husband should treat his wife." (I did look behind him to see if there were wings.)

As I showed him the silk robe inventory, the Lord said to me, "Give him whatever he picks out." I immediately shook my head as if hearing bad news and knew this couldn't be God. Again the Lord said to me, "Give him whatever he picks out." This time it got my attention. I watched the man put a $45 silk chemise with the $115 silk robe he had already placed on the counter. My stomach was flipping at this point. I said (under my breath), "You know, Lord, this sale could pay half the power bill and give some dollars to my employees." I got no reply. I watched the shopper, as he pondered his decision. He finally decided on just the $115 silk robe.

As I was writing up the sale, my head down, focusing on the ticket, I entreated the Lord one last time with, "You know Lord half off wouldn't be bad either?" There was a feeling of disconnect in my spirit, and I knew the answer as I wrote on the ticket—*Jesus paid the price.* The man was shocked and speechless and tried to give the robe back. At which point, I said it didn't belong to me.

After he left, the balance of the day I had my face pressed against the glass on the front door of the shop, as I watched the heavy rain, looking for the thousand-dollar sale that would reflect my obedience to the Lord. The robe "give-a-way" was the only transaction that day.

A few days later, I received a lovely thank-you note from my shopper. He stated that his wife was overjoyed and loved the silk robe, and he prayed that God would bless me a hundred fold. I slipped his thoughtful note into my desk drawer and focused on the urgent issues at hand.

I moved forward in closing and liquidating the business. Meanwhile, my husband was in the hospital recovering from a critical fall. This left me with God to wrap up the details of the shop's closing.

SBA declined my letter of intent to pay off the balance with my statement, "I don't have the funds." This letter was at the direction of my assigned agent who knew my financial picture and said, "This happens with people who have limited funds and SBA would probably put my account in a dead file." Due to my husband's illness and mounting bills, I felt uneasy with this debt hanging over our heads. I wanted closure and my husband agreed.

In the meantime, my parents sent me a thousand dollars to help with the shop expenses—which they had never done in the past. (A year later when recounting to them, their thousand dollar gift, they never remembered sending the money.) When I checked with my SBA agent, he informed me of his transfer to South Carolina. At which time, my account was turned over to another person. He did mention that if SBA saw some type of payment plan, even if it only covered 10 percent of the remaining debt, it might be approved.

My new agent was a lady who was also a past department store buyer, I felt it important to meet her in person. I organized my payment plans for her approval before their Monday meeting for unsecured debt (part of the equity from the condo was already applied to my balance). With my thousand-dollar cushion (which I told no one about), I proposed $400 down and $200 per month for five years.

She knew my background as a department store buyer and we connected. Upon entering her small office, all her walls were lined with large, colorful posters of Panama. She was a native of the Panama Canal Zone, where I was also born. I was getting goose bumps at this point. After laying out my payment proposal, I went home.

She called me the next day with a revamped proposal. She asked me if I could come up with a thousand dollars, she felt she could get my plan approved. After collecting my thoughts, I called to tell her that I indeed had the thousand dollars. The following Monday SBA graciously accepted my thousand dollar offer. I was overjoyed and numb.

Once I signed all the necessary forms at SBA, I began to find closure. As I was driving back to the shop to turn over the keys to the property owner, I began to add up all the debt forgiven from my fashion vendors and SBA in liquidating my business. The *total amount of the debt forgiven was $115,000.*

I immediately went looking for my "note of blessing" from my shopper. I certainly like God's math—a hundred-fold return on a $115 silk robe.

I tell this story to encourage your heart on several points. First, even with a curse operating over my ability to earn an adequate income—God provided a way. In my case, I had to give away a silk robe for a man to speak a blessing over me. This blessing allowed God to by pass the curse—to fulfill the blessing. Second, was the obedience I learned in trusting God when all financial reasoning told me that this decision to give away income (the silk robe) would be a poor one. Third, I learned from God that He would test me in my obedience when I can't "buy my way out." This was just one of many obedience tests with which I would be challenged.

Be encouraged by God's truths on money and finances. Let His truths be a life raft for those challenging times and a warm blanket of peace when the waters are still. His ways never fail. His plans for your life are perfect.

Chapter 9

Roles: Love, Honor, Protect

Lover—The Husband's Role

THE HUSBAND BEING CALLED to be the lover in marriage is no easy request. It bears a responsibility that does not always come easily. This section contains some of God's answers. You may not be conscious of this quest, but your heart is all too familiar with its pain.

If you can admit that you have failed as a lover and admit, "I am guilty" this becomes your biggest step toward healing. This section on *Lover* will require deep reflection and honesty. God knows about the soft, tender places in your heart that have been sealed off. An honest evaluation of your role in the sexual intimacy of your marriage will reveal areas in which you do not give yourself to your bride.

Have you ever noticed the word *lover* refers to the male? It would be hard to read Songs of Solomon without understanding that God has given the male the emotional equipment to be the lover.

Webster's Dictionary defines *lover* as one who cherishes; one who shows passion, devotion, and tenderness.

Consider Song of Solomon, chapter 7. Notice the verbal dialogue Solomon is having with his bride. His Words are filled with passion, devotion, and tenderness.

This verbal passion springs from a heart of passion. God says what is stored in the heart will come forth from our lips. This can be the dipstick test for your heart's heath and its possible need for a tune-up.

After Solomon speaks his heartfelt passion to and over his bride (Song of Solomon 7:1–9), she is intoxicated with his desire for her. In verse ten, her response is, "I am my beloved's and his desire is for me." How did she get to this belief about herself and understanding of her identity in their relationship? Solomon certainly was not thinking his passion to himself. Her husband verbally confirmed her validation, as a desired woman and wife. Only the husband has the authority and anointing to fulfill his wife's need for validation as a woman and assure her that she is passionately loved and desired.

When other men tell me I'm pretty or attractive, it's a nice compliment, but it doesn't convince me of its truth until my husband makes the same declaration. Then I believe I am beautiful—in his eyes. To be desirable in his eyes is the best aphrodisiac. This silent weapon will deliver every time.

If not validated in his person and manhood, husbands often struggle with how to validate their spouse as a woman and wife. It is hard to give love that wasn't given to you first, but this can be a starting place to undo previous lack in your marriage. What was written on your heart growing up? Did you feel you were a blessing to your parents? Did you know they loved you unconditionally without performance? It's OK to be honest and grieve for what should have been. It's being honest in what you believe about yourself as a person, a man, and a son that gives you a big advantage to becoming healed, whole, and loved. Make personal notes to these questions and ponder your answers before God.

Why can't the wife initiate the role of lover? That is not the design God had when he fashioned Eve for Adam. But He gave husbands a willing mate when He said to Eve, "and your desire shall be for your husband" (Gen. 3:16). The wife has the desire. She is just waiting for her lover to say, "You are the only one for me, you complete me, and I need you." What passion is this! And as the husband fulfills his role as a passionate lover, his wife reflects him back to himself as a responding lover.

It requires passion to be a lover! It requires passion to be a godly lover! Being a saved Christian does not make you a passionate lover. Being saved gives you the tools from Christ, which can restore you to be that over-the-top lover in your marriage.

Simply going through the motions in communicating with God will not be the antidote for your lack of ability in this area. In Isaiah 29:13, it is written, "Because this people [God's people] draw near with their words and honor Me with their lip service, but they remove their hearts far from Me, and their reverence for Me consist of tradition learned by rote."

Your relationship of intimacy to your wife is a reflection of your intimacy and relationship with God. It is spiritually impossible to hold your heart closed to your wife and have great passion for God. He says, "How can you say you love Me who you can't see and feel, and not love the person that you can see and feel."

> If someone says, "I love God," and hates his brother, he is a liar; for the one who does not love his brother whom he has seen, cannot love God whom he has not seen.
>
> —1 John 4:20

God knows exactly how He wired your emotions. And this snap-shot of intimacy, passion, and respect toward your wife will clearly be reflected in your relationship with God. This is a vital point to be understood. If you have allowed God to be the lover of your soul, becoming a lover to your bride should be a walk in the park.

These scriptures further punctuate the directional flow of who is the lover:

> And as the bridegroom rejoices over the bride, so your God will rejoice over you.
>
> —ISAIAH 62:5

(Please note, it does not say, "as the bride rejoices over the bride-groom.")

Surprised? In Deuteronomy 24:5, "he [the husband] shall be free at home [from battle] one year and he shall give happiness to his wife." Again, please note the order of God's design, in Proverbs 5:19, "be exhilarated always with her love." Husbands will be exhilarated with the reflection of his passion.

Even men that are earnestly serving God in some ministry or ministry outreach, may lack desire and passion for their wives. This is not OK with God. Escaping the obligation to provide intimacy and passion to your wife in no way reflects God. This is not how He loves. Our passionate loving God wants His persona reflected through you to those around you, especially your wife.

We have explored earlier, God's wisdom on cleaving. Being a lover is another dimension of this intimacy. Films portraying an aggres-sive, attractive woman tearing the shirt off the male do not portray a realistic picture of true, intimate fulfillment but present a picture of lust. Great sex does not necessarily make a great lover. A lover validates his wife as a woman and cherishes her life. As her lover, you would nourish your wife and fill her emotional cup to overflowing and intoxicate her with your love.

Cherishing and nourishing are how the Lord describes His passion and love for the body of Christ. This command is set down as an example for the husbands to follow in loving their wives. Ephesians 5:29 says, "For no one ever hated his own flesh, but nourishes and cherishes it, just as Christ also does the church." Note the same statement earlier in Ephesians 5:25 that, "Husbands, love your wives, just as Christ also loved the church." Christ left this example for the husbands to follow. Christ is calling the husband to love his wife by cherishing her and nourishing her—just as Christ cherishes and nourishes His followers.

Webster's Dictionary defines cherish (verb) as: to hold dear; treat with care and affection; to keep deeply in mind. *Cherish* is a verb, an action word. Cherish is a word whose definition can only be understood by action, as reflected by the person who commits to cherishing another. To cherish your wife, you demonstrate your love by your actions toward her. Cherishing is motivated and expressed by tender communication and not by rote, or it is not authentic.

Your wife needs to hear the words, spoken or in written form, about your deep affections for her and that you are always concerned for her happiness, peace of mind, and contentment. What stops men from fulfilling their role as a Solomon lover and expressing pleasure with their wife?

The word *nourish* is defined as: (verb) to promote the growth or development of.

Here again, is another verb that requires action for its definition to be fulfilled.

Husband: the verb definition is to manage prudently.

Husband-man: farmer

Husbandry: the control or judicious use of resources; agriculture.

Christ is saying that the husband, in becoming the Christ-like lover to his wife, will nourish her for her full growth and development. That is emotionally, physically, and spiritually, as a farmer nourishes his crops so they flourish and develop to their maximum potential under his care.

Father God tells us why and how He called the husband to be the lover in the marriage. The husband is to cherish and nourish his wife. These two words—cherish and nourish—are used exclusively only here in Ephesians 5:29, and these two words are not listed to describe agape love in 1 Corinthians 13. Jesus Christ is clarifying in Ephesians 5:29 that the passion He has for the body of Christ is only matched by this same passion a man should have for his wife.

Husbands perhaps are thinking they could use some cherishing and nourishing themselves. How can this conflict be resolved? The good news is you can give new information to your heart that says, "I am loved and I am wonderful."

Father God foreknew you, and He is mindful of every detail of your life. From the first moment of your existence, your birth, to this present time, He is intimately aware of every detail of your pain, hurt, and disappointments. He has made a way for your restoration.

Please read the entire Psalm 139, and let His truth wash over your spirit. Read it every day until your heart believes it. Do not skimp here—this is vital. Read it aloud so as to get a double blessing, by speaking it and then by hearing it. It says in Romans 10:17, "So faith comes from hearing, and hearing by the word of Christ." You will know when your heart receives this scripture as truth. All permanent changes of behavior start first in the heart, for out of the heart flows the issues of life. God's reflection in you will establish your new life-giving dialogue—spoken from your lips.

Your parents may not have been mindful of your emotional needs to be loved and validated, but your heavenly Father provided a way in His Word to let you know that imperfect, careless parents are no substitution for His love and watchful eye over your life. Your life matters to God and He grieves that you were not shown love by your parents and that your existence was not validated. God has not taken His eye off of you. You are the apple of His eye. He has a purpose and plan for your life because He planned it. Trust Him.

To forgive our parents for their imperfect love or careless regard for our emotional well-being, it helps to pray a prayer of forgiveness. It can be a simple prayer, but to bring deliverance, it must come from the heart.

Prayer of Forgiveness

Father God, my heart hurts because of the lack of love and validation from my parents. Their lack of love defined me as being unimportant and of little value.

I hated them for their lack of nurturing and care, and I then hated myself for being unlovable and not worthy to be loved.

Father God, forgive me for the hate that I feel justified to hold in my heart towards my parents or parent for all the ways they made me feel unloved and unlovable. I forgive you Mom and/or Dad for all the ways you made me feel unloved and unlovable. I forgive you for your lack of nurture and care in my life. Father God, I ask that you forgive my parents for all the pain and emotional harm they gave me by withholding their love from me. I ask this in Jesus name. Amen.

Father God, you say in Your Word that whatever I ask, according to Your will, it will be granted unto me. Because You say, You are a father to the orphan, I ask you Father God, to re-parent me and give me the love and validation that You intended for me to receive from my parents. Let me feel Your validation and love. I ask this in Jesus' name. Amen.

These prayers can be adapted and changed to fit situations in your formative years. The Holy Spirit will bring all the details back to your remembrance as you pray and forgive.

How many times did Jesus tell the sick, the lame and the demon-possessed that their sins were forgiven? Forgiveness is a powerful ally. It keeps us humble and doesn't allow the actions of another to crimp, defile, or destroy our life's purpose. Forgiveness can become a daily exercise in our life, especially when we realize the person we withhold forgiveness from, is not even mindful that they have hurt us. Forgiveness never comes too late with God.

A spiritual principle often overlooked when seeking to discover what could be sabotaging your ability to fully love is explained by Jesus in Matthew 7:1–2, "Do not judge so that you will not be judged. For in the way you judge, you will be judged; and by your standard of measure, it will be measured to you." Mark 4:24 says, "Take care what you listen to. By your standard of measure, it shall be measured to you; and more shall be given you besides."

Judging another's choices, behavior, and actions, brings forth the same consequences in our life. Scripture says that as we judge another, we will exhibit that same demeanor in our behavior.

If you often judged your father, in your heart, with bitterness for a behavior or action you disliked or hated, you, in time, will reap this judgment. It will pour over your heart and you will exhibit the same nasty habits and actions you judged once you are married, because you judged your father as a married man. And if your son judges you and becomes you, does he really become his grandfather? Sin seldom loses its way.

Husbands, if you angrily told yourself, consciously or subconsciously, "I hate my father. I never want to be like my father. My father is a loser," you will become your father, the day you say, "I do." With this judgment, you get the whole package of who and what your father is. You get the seen and unseen. As children, we are not wise enough to judge their actions, so we judge the person. These seeds of judgment will wait for the appropriate harvest time to bring forth its fruit. Hebrews 12:15 says, "See to it that no one comes short of the grace of God; that no root of bitterness springing up causes trouble, and by it many be defiled."

Story

Friends of ours were eagerly awaiting their marriage. He had been married once before and she had also been married before. I shared the above principle of judgment with them both, attempting to forewarn them of consequences of failing to address problems in their prior failed marriages, which could replay in their pending marriage. I guess love is not only blind, but also deaf (I think most of us have been there). My counsel on taking care of past business was not heeded or perhaps, not understood. I warned them that when the "I do" is said, the consequences of past judgments not dealt with from their early formative years and past marriages, will fall to the current marriage relationship. The fulfillment of the immutable law of judging, sowing, and reaping will begin. These immutable laws are impartial. They carry out its self-fulfilling mission—good or bad. There are no voids in God's kingdom.

In meeting with the wife a few weeks after their honeymoon, she seemed hurt and confused. In her anguish, which reflected her frustration in her marriage, she said, "We elected to have a small wedding with only a few family members and friends. After the ceremony and a quiet short reception, we left for our honeymoon destination. He put me in the car. By the time he walked around to the driver's side, a different man got into the car. And *that* man has been with me ever since."

These folks have had many heated challenges in their marriage, and communication has failed them almost every time. God's laws are clear. Our failure to believe in these laws will not negate the consequences of breaking them.

It is important to understand facets of judging we may have used for self-protection. God is the only judge. With this understanding we can unravel these tentacles of past judgments off our lives and off our marriages.

What will be required of you for this deliverance from judgment will be your honesty. With pen and paper, in a quiet space, evaluate what judgments you could have declared to your heart in anger against your father. Hang onto this list and apply it to the prayers below.

Prayer to Destroy Judgment

Father God, I recognize that You are the only Judge and I have sinned greatly against You by judging one of Your children, my father. My posture in judging my father was also dishonoring. Therefore, Father God I ask in the name of Jesus, my Lord and Savior, that You forgive me for judging my father. When I declared in anger, "I never wanted to be like him," but that You would grant me favor and deliverance from this judgment(s)_____.

As only You can Father God, I ask that You would restore me to the original plan You have for my life's purpose. Give me ears to hear the sins of my mouth, and keep a muzzle over my lips so I don't fall into judgment. Let me always be conscious to obey your commandments, in Jesus' name. Amen.

Forgiveness

I forgive you Dad for all the hurtful, unkind, and insensitive ways you role modeled your life in front of me. I forgive you for your lack of nurturing and validation towards me as I was growing up. I forgive you, Dad, for all the ways you caused me to sin against you and to dishonor you and God by my hateful judgments. I forgive you Dad for the pain. Amen.

I put the Cross of Calvary between my Dad and myself and I nail to the cross my judgment I made that I never want to be like my Dad—in any way. I declare in the name of Jesus this judgment destroyed and inoperative in my life from this day forth. Amen.

Sowing and Reaping

Father God, I ask in the name of Jesus that you would destroy any further reaping of these "judgment seeds" that I planted in my heart—for all the many times I judged my father. I ask for divine favor in releasing me from any further reaping of consequences, due to my hateful judgments of my Dad. I also ask that you would forgive my Dad for all his unkind hurtful ways that caused me to judge him and for the sin of this judgment to stop with my generation. Amen.

Let God's Word be a mantle of truth around your heart. He knows every detail of your pain, hurt, and disappointment. God did not leave you an orphan. He sent His Son, Jesus Christ, to take the sting of our sins to the Cross.

Honor—The Husband's Role

God has called you to honor your wife. Why has God called the husband to give to his wife due honor? And what does that word convey? Let's consult *Webster's Dictionary. It* defines honor:

Honor (noun): good name, reputation; outward respect, a person of superior standing, used esp. as a title; one that brings respect and fame.

Honor (verb): to regard or treat with honor, to confer honor on.

What is Father God's definition of honor? God was careful to choose the word honor over the word respect. The meaning of respect is not unimportant, but usually respect must be earned. In the case of honor, it is not earned because it's the position held that is to be honored.

When God gave Moses the Ten Commandments He said, "Honor your father and mother" (Exod. 20:12). In 1 Peter 3:7, the apostle Peter states, "live with your wives in an understanding way, as with a weaker vessel, since she is a woman; and grant her honor as a fellow heir of the grace of life."

When God states and commands you to honor your parents and wife, there is usually a consequence if you do not comply. When we dishonor our parents, it will not go well for us in the area in which we dishonor them. As you dishonor your wife, your prayers are hindered or go unheard. Therefore, to honor someone as God commands is not negotiable. It does not imply that you have to respect this person, though in honoring them, you would reflect a respectful demeanor.

My Bible defines honor as: to esteem or regard highly (NASB).

God entreats us, "If you love Me, honor Me with your life. If you abide in My Commandments and My Word, they will bring you life and not death. Giving you rains in season and not famine, and you will reflect My Son Jesus Christ, who learned obedience by the things He suffered."

The apostle John states in John 5:23, "He who does not honor the Son does not honor the Father who sent Him."

When we don't honor our parents, or dishonor our wife, we show dishonor to God. This brings bad fruit and frustration. This dishonoring posture only changes as your heart's attitude toward honoring changes. It is important then to know why God holds these relationships in such high honor. Therefore, understanding and knowledge are great catalysts to change.

How do you dishonor your wife? A starting place is to ask her. She will tell you everything. And husbands do not begrudge her ability to remember the finite details of her issues with you. Be grateful that it's specific and not general. General prayers never moved the heart of God. When confessing sin, you need to be specific so that specific sin can be blotted out of the Book of Life under your name. You will be accountable before God for all the deeds done in the body and for every careless word you speak.

You may know how to apologize, but the people in your world may not. Do you hold that grudge in your heart and strip them of their honor because of their inability to apologize. For your parents, you know the prayer of forgiveness that needs to be said. It's a little trickier with your wife, as your relationship with your wife is a reflection of your relationship with God.

Once you have the list from your wife, ask for her prayer support and agreement that as you lift your dishonoring behavior up to the Lord that He will put His axe to the root and destroy your dishonoring behavior toward her. Perhaps your father was dishonoring to your mother. Forgive him. Write out the prayer and say it until you are free of that judgment in your heart. Your wife has extra "sonar" from God, and she will be able to detect the bite in your words until this work is done in your heart and the judgments you made are destroyed.

Do not belittle your wife if she attempts to help and comes across as your Holy Spirit. The wives will have a very clear understanding in their section of God's role for them in this area. In the meantime, pray for her and her frustration. After all, she is only trying to help in the healing process. Find a kind way to express your annoyance. Her heart may have pure but misguided motives in trying to help. Your encouragement could be the antidote to her silence.

As you pray and seek God for deliverance and healing, you can structure in your mind ways to honor your wife. You can ask her in what ways you could change to show her honor.

In my frustration to understand the dishonoring chaos in the early part of my marriage, I read every book written by a favorite Christian author and listened to some of his early tapes on marriage. I needed answers and was frustrated. He gave testimony of how his marriage was restored in the midst of not knowing there was a problem until his wife had had enough, was willing to quit, and voiced her complaint. As he listened to her complaints of dishonor, he implemented the needed changes to save his marriage and found his mission and passion with God forever changed. Today, because of his newfound passion, he has become a best-selling author on marriage and family issues—because of the providence of God and a brave wife.

A Pastor's Story

He was a youth pastor for his church and his home was adjacent. He would often walk home for lunch. He would go to the kitchen, greet his wife, and sit at the kitchen table to have his lunch. This day was different. His wife had his lunch on the table but she still had her back to him, and she stood motionless at the sink. In asking what was wrong, without turning around she stated in a very cold, unemotional tone that she had had it. She would continue to live in their home, raise their children, and prepare the meals, but the marriage was over.

Shocked and dumbfounded, he never had the first clue that his wife was so unhappy (and he did a very brave and wise thing next). He stated that he was not going to leave that kitchen table until she told him *everything*. Confident by the tone of his voice that he was genuine, she told him all the ways he dishonored her in front of the children and how some of his playful actions towards the children dishonored them. This went on for hours as he took copious notes.

This encounter changed his interest from youth pastor to family and marriage counseling. He was intent on stopping the damage he had done to his wife and family. He purposed to go deep into God's Word to bring victory in restoring his wife to her place of honor and restore his children's hearts from his actions of dishonoring them. Because of his heart to please God, God blessed him.

There is no telling what God has in store for men who humble themselves under His leadership. You may find yourself choosing different friends because of their careless behavior towards their wives. Or, you may feel led to be an example of change as they watch the ways you honor your wife. The next time you dine with friends and your wife excuses herself, stand up and pull out her chair. As you continue socializing at the table, watch for her return. As she walks toward the table, stand and seat her again. Your wife will feel honored and will glow. How does it feel to be your wife's hero? Could it be because she can't stop smiling?

Why do you dishonor your wife? Changing how your actions are dishonoring will not bring honor until the why is dealt with. When the why is answered, freedom comes and actions of honoring will follow naturally.

The *why* I dishonor my wife:

1. My mother showed disrespect toward me when I was growing up.

2. My father dishonored my mother.

3. A woman of authority in my life showed disrespect toward me.

1. My mother showed disrespect toward me growing up.

> *Mother, I forgive you for all the many ways that you showed me disrespect (fill in the blank) _____.*
> *I forgive you for all the ways you made me feel unworthy and insufficient. And Father God, in Jesus' name, I ask that You forgive my mother for her actions and words of disrespect towards me and that You destroy the consequences of her judgments from my life. Amen.*
>
> *Father God, I ask in Jesus' name that You would forgive me for holding this resentment of dishonor toward my mother in my heart. Create in me a pure heart and renew a right spirit in me. Forgive me for all the ways I was dishonoring to my mother in my words, my actions, and in my thoughts. I nail to the cross of Calvary this "root" of my dishonoring, and I give you, Father God, my pain, disappointment, and hurt. I ask that You would restore my wounded spirit to its natural function of showing honor to women. Amen.*

2. My father was dishonoring to my mother.

I forgive you father (dad), for all the ways you dishonored mom, which caused me to judge you and follow suit in my own marriage. I forgive you father for being a poor example of an honoring, loving husband. Father God, I ask in Jesus' name, that you forgive my father for all the many ways he dishonored my mother and taught me, by example, to do likewise. Restore honor to my father's heart toward my mother. Amen.

Father God, I ask in Jesus' name, that You would forgive me for judging my father's behavior of dishonor towards my mother. By that judgment, I condemned myself to those same actions (Romans 2:1). I ask Father God, that in Your loving kindness and mercy towards me, that You would annul the consequences of my judgments that caused my actions to be dishonoring to my wife, and I ask Lord Jesus, that this "root of dishonor" be forever destroyed in my heart. In Jesus' name. Amen.

3. A woman of authority in my life showed disrespect toward me.

For the woman or women who showed you disrespect, use prayer number one (above) and insert her name instead of mother. Again, these prayers are a guideline. Restructure these to fit your personal situation.

Nothing really happens in your heart until there is confession; a petition to Father God for forgiveness; and repentance for those actions. This process softens your heart to trust yourself to honor. This may not be an overnight experience. Remember, for all the many times you spoke lies to your heart, you will need to restate truth instead of those lies you have believed about yourself and women to a statement of truth about yourself and your special woman-of-honor—your wife.

Some husbands are fathers of sons who watch their every move, voice tone, action, and response. Be mindful that you not to pass dishonoring onto the next generation. If you have/had a father you didn't want to reflect in your marriage, find the appropriate prayer and stick with it until the reflection is changed. Proverbs 20:7, "A righteous man who walks in his integrity, how blessed are his sons after him." Now is your chance to bless your son's future. You can stop this dishonoring with your generation.

It is a man of great integrity who honors. Honoring your wife in the audience of friends and children may separate you from the crowd, but Jesus stated often in the Gospels that the way to heaven is a narrow path and not many take it. Being popular with God can leave you unpopular with some of your friends. Be unpopular, honor your wife and hold her in high regard. After all, she's the one who kisses you goodnight.

Protector—The Husband's Role

God made the husband and gifted the husband as the protector of his wife and family. No "knight in shinning armor" is required for this role. The real test is the peace that lives in his home.

Webster's Dictionary defines the following:

Protect (verb): to shield from injury, guard

Protector (noun): one that protects

Protection (noun): the state of being protected—the supervision or support of one that is smaller or weaker

Protection is divided into two categories—physical and spiritual. God defines these categories as a man's responsibility and role as husband.

Physical Protection

You husbands in the same way, live with your wives in an understanding way, as with someone weaker, since she is a woman.

—1 PETER 3:7

God designed the woman physically weaker than the man. The wife is physically weaker than the husband and will tire more easily. It's your role to protect your wife from over exhaustion. Don't advise your wife to stop all the needed physical work she is doing in and around the house, but do some of the strenuous heavy work for her or have someone else do it. You know the physical maintenance your house requires. Part of your protection involves protecting the home you provided for your family. Keeping the house physically safe is the man's responsibility.

A Story

My late husband, Michael, in the early years of our marriage took his 6 a.m. jog around the grounds of our condo and left the door unlocked! I told him how frightening that was for me because I was still sleeping, and anyone could come in and harm me. In expressing my fear, I heard a casual response from Michael with little change. One day, a unit adjacent to our condominium complex had news of a woman raped at 7 a.m., as she stepped out of her shower. She had opened her sliding door on her second floor balcony apartment before stepping into the shower. The rapist was never caught. Michael then locked the door when he went for his runs. Whatever frightens a wife, she counts on her husband for protection from any form of harm—physical, emotional, or verbal. Protect your wife.

Genesis 3:16 says, "and he shall rule over you." God is informing Eve, in the presence of Adam, that He holds Adam responsible for the well-being and safety of Eve. God's translation to Eve, "Rest in the assurance that Adam will keep you from harm's way, and you will not have to protect yourself because I have armed, fortified, and anointed your husband for this role." Your protection is very important for your wife's sense of security. You are the one she depends on. If you fall short in this role, recall how your father lacked in protecting your mother. If there is a similar pattern between you and your father, pray the forgiveness prayer.

Spiritual Protection

Scriptures in which Jesus explained the importance of the husband's authority as his wife's spiritual protector, are stated three times—in Matthew, Mark, and Luke. I have selected the scripture from Luke to exemplify this.

> When a strong man fully armed, guards his own house, his possessions are undisturbed. But when someone else stronger than he attacks him and over powers him, he takes away from him all his armor on which he relied and distributes his plunder.
>
> —LUKE 11:21–22

Just how does this happen? Who is the someone else that is stronger? And why does this someone need to take the entire armor? According to Ephesians 6:13–17, the pieces of armor have, "girded your loins with truth, having put on the breastplate of righteousness, and having shod your feet with the preparation of the gospel of peace, the shield of faith, helmet of salvation, the sword of the Spirit." They were designed by God for protection on every front. How does the enemy have permission then to strip the husband of his armor?

The *someone else* mentioned in detail in the verse above, is defined in Ephesians 6:12, which states, "For our struggle is not against flesh and blood, but against the rulers, against the powers, against the world forces of this darkness, against the spiritual forces of wickedness in the heavenly places." These are Satan and all of his fallen angels (demons). Therefore, *someone else* refers to Satan.

The strongman is you, the husband, and you will be under attack by those spiritual forces. Satan and his demons will try to find the legal, unrepented ground in your life, which allows them to strip you of your armor. This will leave the door open for Satan to conquer your wife, family and finances. These forces try to divide and conquer. Keeping you and your wife divided is part of Satan's plan to conquer and destroy your marriage along with the call on your life.

Satan knows the lies we believe that can keep us twisted in a knot for years. He sees us lie, cheat, and steal. He has observed us over the years and delights in whispering those nasty reminders in our ear. His goal is to make us believe that we are not worth much to the Kingdom of God. He intends to destroy the marriage that God has put together. If Satan defeats the strongman, he destroys the family's protection.

God has provided ways for you to fight this invisible foe. Understanding the importance of the armor of God gives God the responsibility of overseeing His Word to perform it (Jeremiah 1:12).

God stated in Isaiah 43:26, "put Me in remembrance of My word." Reading aloud this scripture for putting on the armor of God carries many protection benefits. A suggested prayer to read over yourself, your wife, and your family member—Ephesians 6:14–17 (author's paraphrase):

> *I put on the full armor of God that I may be able to resist the devil and his evil plans. I gird my loins with truth, put on the breastplate of righteousness, and with the shoes of peace, I take up the shield of faith and put on the helmet of salvation and take up the sword of the Word of God. I also put this armor over my wife and family members. Amen.*

This should be part of getting dressed every morning. It is wise to teach this prayer to your wife and children. What a wonderful way to teach your family and encourage them that God is our source of strength and protection. It comforts them as they look to you as their protector.

Let us understand the function of each part of the armor for how and why it was designed by God to bring that protection against the enemy for you and your family members. This clearer understanding will have long-term benefits.

1. "Gird your loins with truth."

"To prepare oneself for strenuous effort"—as defined by *Reader's Digest Encyclopedia Dictionary*. It also goes on to state that the loins are the reproductive organs. Thus, the apostle Paul in Ephesians 6:14, leads us into a true understanding of our heritage. Truthfully evaluate your childhood roots, and deal with those tough issues in the light of truth so legal ground isn't established, opening the door to the enemy. Any bitterness, hatred, or inability to forgive over unfinished business with your father and mother must go to the cross-stopping passage.

Act 8:23 says, "For you see that you are in the gall of bitterness and in bondage of iniquity"—translated—"For I see you are living in your bitterness and in bondage of sin."

2. "Put on the breastplate of righteousness."

The breastplate protects the heart. Your heart will bless or destroy your relationship with your wife, family members, and others.

Inventory the spiritual contents of your heart because your mouth will betray you and set your life on fire as Satan is gleefully applauding. It might explain those ongoing negative issues in your marriage and at your workplace. Or, read the book of Job and see Satan's working knowledge of the Word of God.

3. "Shod your feet with the gospel of peace."

When your spirit is saturated with the Word of God, His peace follows. As you mirror that peace to your wife and family members they know they are safe. God's peace gives stability and a sense of well-being. Only the husband can guard his marriage and home with such peace. Hosea 4:6 says, "My people are destroyed for lack of knowledge," and that is what the enemy is counting on—your ignorance.

4. "The shield of faith."

The shield of faith will allow you to extinguish all the flaming missiles of the evil one. Shield yourself and your family from the lies the evil one throws at you. The antidote is faith. "Faith comes from hearing, and hearing the Word of God" (Rom. 10:17). Do you attend church often to hear the Word of God? Do you read the Word aloud in your home? Has your faith been tested? Did you win or fail? Joseph, Jacob's son, was a dreamer and a man of great faith. He was tested in every area in which men are tested. The story of Joseph is one of my favorites. (See Genesis 37–47.)

Faith is built from one struggle to the next, one challenge to the next, and the only force that can neutralize the enemy is our faith in God. Lift your shield around your marriage and family and be courageous.

5. "The helmet of salvation."

The helmet of salvation protects your mind and thoughts from the lies of the enemy and from unhealthy non-spiritual food upon which you graze. These might be provocative TV programs, or listening to provocative words or music. Protect your thoughts and be selective of what you feed your mind for the sake of entertainment. The enemy knows the flesh is weak and wants to plant those ungodly thoughts into your mind. He knows that eventually, such words and statements will roll off your lips. The enemy knows well God's Word and knows "we shall have what we confess with our mouth." When Satan tested Jesus in the wilderness, Jesus answered Satan with Scripture—every time.

This helmet of salvation belongs to all born-again believers. However, you need to protect what you allow to come into your mind, as well as that of your wife and family members. Your wife and family will follow your lead. Don't correct your daughter for wearing provocative clothing and then allow her to watch provocative TV and movies, or worst yet, see you watching them. God sets you to be the standard in your marriage because if the enemy takes you down—Satan gets the whole family. Be reminded of the battles in the Old Testament when the king was captured or killed. The battle was won by the opposing army, no matter how many men were left on either side. Satan, the enemy, is after the "king" in the family—the husband.

6. "The sword of the Spirit" is the Word of God.

The Word of God is your only offensive weapon against the enemy. Are you aware that Satan knows the Word of God verbatim? Do you know the Word of God verbatim? Be encouraged with some favorite scriptures, which keep us mindful of the power of the sword of the Word and how it works.

> You have seen well, for I [God] am watching over My word to perform it.
> —JEREMIAH 1:12

> So will My word be which goes forth from My mouth; It will not return to Me empty, without accomplishing what I desire.
> —ISAIAH 55:11

> Put Me in remembrance [of My word]; let us argue our case together; State your cause, that you may be proved right.
> —ISAIAH 43:26

> Bless the Lord, you His angels, mighty in strength, who perform His Word, obeying the voice of His Word.
> —PSALM 103:20

> Do you not know that we will judge angels?
> —1 CORINTHIANS 6:3

The first four scriptures give us the same message. God's Word is never ignored, either by Him or by His angels. In rightfully handling the Word of God, you can destroy the works of the evil one in your life, marriage, and family. And in the last scripture, 1 Corinthians 6:3, we will judge our angels—later.

Husbands are much more clever at war games then we women. As you prepare for battle, closely examine your offensive and defensive weapons by which you can conquer the enemy. You can exercise often with these weapons of warfare until you master your technique in handling them to your advantage. This is also true with the Word of God. Master the Word of God, know the Word of God, match the Word of God to your situation, call out the Word of God as your battle cry, conquer the enemy and be unmovable.

Man's role as protector, is built into his nature by the Master Planner—God. Stand up to your full stature and reclaim your marriage and family. Be your wife's hero. You are the only one suited and anointed for that role.

Joy's Story of Protection

In December 1983, my new designer lingerie shop was open in time for Christmas business. The first nine months were uneventful with many changes and revamped strategies to increase revenue. Ten months later, in early October, my security company awakened me at 3 a.m., reporting a break-in at my shop. To my disappointment, the robbers had hand-selected only the designer and silk lingerie as their target. The items that were my biggest sellers for Christmas business were gone.

Later, in talking with my Christian friend, Karen, she asked, "Are you not praying Psalm 91 over your shop the entire inventory?" I thought this was no time for a Bible lesson, but I did ponder her comment. Though I was an avid reader of the Word, as a new believer, I was not as familiar with the Old Testament. After locating Psalm 91, I began to read it aloud every morning over the shop and inventory. Also, the employee who opened the shop was required to read Psalm 91 aloud before opening the doors to the public.

Six months later my faith in God's Word was tested—with another break-in at 3:30 a.m. As I was returning home from my vandalized shop, with its new plywood panel concealing the broken front window, I was having a strong discussion with God. I was reminding Him that, "His store just got robbed and His angels were asleep and didn't stop it." I was very upset and confused. Unmarried, with parents I kept in the dark about my many challenges at the shop, I felt so alone. I just wanted some peace and protection.

The phone was ringing as I entered the house. It was the man from the Security Company at cobblestone mall. He said, "We just found a pile of lingerie at the side of the building. It looks like something or someone frightened the robbers and they dropped the merchandise in a hurry. Can you come and identify the lingerie?"

Yes, every piece was accounted for. And the something that frightened them? You got it. It was a couple of very tall angels. May I tell you how worn out the Psalm 91 page is in my Bible! God's angels were overseeing His Word to perform it.

As a footnote, my shop was moved to an enclosed mall for four years and then I moved it back to the original location, under new management. Two months after re-opening, there was another break in, and yes, four days later we found the merchandise in a pile behind the building. I keep my angels very busy.

In reading Psalm 91 aloud since that October 1984 break-in, I continue today. I call it out over my family members, home, car, business, and planes when traveling. My late husband also would read Psalm 91 aloud over us until, due to his illness, he lost his ability to speak.

I soon realized that I would be tested, and my faith increased as I allowed God's challenges to shape my confidence in His ability to perform His Word. It feels like a big, warm blanket of peace. You can blanket your wife and family in this same peace as you arm yourself with the Word of God to protect them. With each challenge you face, your desire for more of His Word will increase your appetite for victory.

For your convenience, I have provided Psalm 91 (NIV):

> He who dwells in the shelter of the Most High will rest in the shadows of the Almighty. I will say of the Lord, "He is my refuge and my fortress, my God, in whom I trust." Surely he will save you from the fowler's snare and from the deadly pestilence. He will cover you with his feathers, and under his wings you will find refuge; his faithfulness will be your shield and rampart. You will not feel the terror of night, nor the arrow that flies by day, nor the pestilence that stalks in the darkness, nor the plague that destroys at midday. A thousand may fall at your side, ten thousand at your right hand, but it will not come near you. You will only observe with your eyes and see the punishment of the wicked. If you make the Most High your dwelling—even the Lord, who is my refuge—then no harm will befall you; no disaster will come near your tent. For he will command his angels concerning you to guard you in all your ways; they will lift you up in their hands, so that you will not strike your foot against a stone. You will tread upon the lion and the cobra; you will trample the great lion and the serpent. "Because he loves me," says the Lord, "I will rescue him; I will protect him, for he acknowledges my name. He will call upon me, and I will answer him; I will be with him in trouble, I will deliver him and honor him. With long life will I satisfy him and show him my salvation."

As you arm yourself with the Word of God and speak His Word, the enemy will flee, and the fruits of peace and prosperity will come. This may all be very new to you. I know what new feels like, but if I can muster up the strength to save my little shop from the threats of the enemy—you, blessed husband, can protect your family with one hand tied.

Summary—Husband

Husbands, let us recap the three rules and three roles that God has appointed to you, along with a passion, to aid in fulfilling its purpose. Passion is a powerful companion, which intensifies the color and sounds of your life. Interestingly enough, when one has a passion for what is required of him, he performs it without effort and is filled with great joy in its accomplishment. Passion is the drive that defines your purpose, while at the same time, fires up your desire for more. Being passionate about your responsibilities in a marriage can be very contagious.

God's rules for husbands are:
Cleave
Authority
Provider

God's roles for husbands are:
Lover
Honor
Protector

What I witnessed in my own marriage and other Christian marriages, is when the husband is unable to perform in one of the rules, he can still perform in one or both of the other two areas. For example, he may not be able to cleave and be intimate with his wife, but he could be a good provider. I have also witnessed marriages where the husband, due to the high stressful dynamics in his formative years, failed in all three rules.

In the area of roles, I have often witnessed the very opposite. If the husband fails in one of the roles, he usually fails in all three. This makes it a very stressful marriage for both spouses, and leaves them feeling powerless to bring about change. Fortunately, you now know the truth and what is required of you. If you can't love, honor, or protect your wife, it most often has to do with her being a woman. That is usually the result of your first encounter with a female (usually mom). Or perhaps, your father didn't love, honor, or protect your mother, and you became your father. You know what to do and what God requires. You have the prayers for freedom. It is worth the effort. Remember, God believes in you.

In the Books of Jeremiah, Isaiah, Psalms and others, Father God speaks to His people, Israel, through His prophets, reminding them how He saved them from extinction. He showed His great passion for His people as He took them from labor camps in Egypt and led them safely out of Egypt with great wealth—loaded down with silver and gold. He protected them by drowning the enemy in the Red Sea. He gave His people wisdom and direction as He guided them with His pillar of cloud by day and His pillar of fire by night. He fed them supernaturally and gave them water to drink. He listened to their complaints and adjusted His course to accommodate. He forgave them their sins of the heart and sins in deeds done. He preserved their life and fought their enemies. He showed them how passionately and unconditionally He loved them, by forgiving them again and again. He fulfilled His promises to them. He delivered those who stayed close to Him with their heritage in the promise land, while fighting their enemies for clear passage. He gave them the land of milk and honey for their pleasure and reward.

The scripture further tells us:

> Behold, days are coming, declares the Lord, when I will make a new covenant with the house of Israel and with the house of Judah, not like the covenant which I made with their fathers. In the day I took them by the hand to bring them out of the land of Egypt, My covenant, which they broke, although I was a husband to them, declares the Lord.
> —JEREMIAH 31:31–32

Father God chose this metaphor to give a complete understanding of what He requires of a husband. Father God gave His people miracle after miracle. The husband is anointed to be that miracle worker in his family. Father God is the perfect role model. Father God fed, protected, guided, fought their battles, granted favor, listened to their complaints, loved them unconditionally, and forgave His people over and over again. This is God's perspective on what He requires of a husband.

Husbands, may God richly bless you in every area of your life, marriage, and workplace! Be kind to yourself and relax. Your relationship with Father God is the greatest asset in your marriage. You make the wheels turn, the music play, and the laughter flow or not flow in your marriage. God designed and made you first, for His great pleasure and purpose. Find God, find yourself, find your passion, and everything else will be drawn unto you.

> Enjoy life with the woman whom you love all the days of your fleeting life which He has given to you under the sun; for

this is your reward in life, and in your toil in which you have labored under the sun.

—ECCLESIASTES 9:9

Part IV

Wife

An excellent wife, who can find? For her worth is far above jewels.

—PROVERBS 31:10

Chapter 10

Rules: Helper, Desire, Submit

L ADIES, THIS IS OUR time to bring into sharper focus God's plan for women and wives. I have worked for a large company, owned my own business, and was a stay-at-home wife, caring for a sick husband while handling a home-based business. I can't really say which role I liked best—perhaps the role that caused me to depend most on God.

I took my position and responsibility in my marriage with a heart to please God and with a posture of respect toward my husband. As you have read, I had a challenging marriage from the start. He knows how I love to connect the dots and sharpen my mind for the challenges of the quest. The quest being, "Why is this marriage not working?"

My thoughts on being a mom betrayed me to believe I had all the time in the world for motherhood. I admire mothers and the role you play in the young lives entrusted to them. Especially with males, mothers can impact their son's heart in ways that can change how he views women and the respect or disrespect he will later show them.

Understanding the boundaries in your marriage is godly wisdom. This wisdom, however, may not be the shorter route, but it is by far the only route that brings change. Understanding your limitations and responsibilities in marriage and the family unit, however, sometimes involves making tougher, inconvenient life choices.

We women are not our husband's Holy Spirit or God. And wisdom comes in knowing when to share and when to pray. If the proportion is not at least 50-percent share and 50-percent prayer, conflicts will occur in your marriage. I've been there—way too many times. Though I believe myself to be a convincing speaker and conveyor of deep concepts, it did not help my execution when voicing solutions to my husband about our challenging marital issues. I found praying before speaking to my husband heightened his ability to hear me. This wisdom came after much trial and error.

We will embark on an adventure that can change your life and your thoughts; and destroy the lies you may believe about men. Your race in your marriage may never have started; perhaps you have been running in place for years, hoping to find the way to the finish line.

We women are part of God's original plan. He fashioned us out of living, organic material—Adam's rib. We were purposed and hand-designed for our husband's great pleasure. It sounds likes a big job requirement. Not with God, He has equipped us for our role as women and wives. We just need to use wisdom. Proverbs 11:22 says, "As a ring of gold in a swine's snout, so is a beautiful woman who lacks discretion."

Some wives have chosen to survive in their marriage, with no desire to upset the cart. I understand your pain of rejection and loneliness. God understands your pain even better and doesn't want you to quit. You are the only one, other then God, who knows the details of the emotional pain and challenges your husband faces daily in your marriage. God is counting on you to do your part. Each wife expresses her pain, hurt, disappointment, and loneliness differently, but each needs to run her race according to God's standards.

What God first requires of us is honesty in evaluating our marriage relationship and then mapping out actions based on His truth. Denial never made a marriage better, and in most cases, confuses the husband as to how well he is doing in the marriage. Husbands often don't understand the cause of their wife's actions and moods—cool, distant, moody, rote kindness, and more, because most husbands don't equate her negative reactions as reflections of their own negative behavior. Your husband's inability to understanding your moods may be due to his void of emotional intimacy with you, therefore, he is unable to *feel* your spirit. Denial says, "Intimacy will never happen in my marriage so why try? I'll take care of myself and call my marriage by a name suitable and acceptable that we both can find livable." You just told God you don't need His help.

It's easy to understand the dynamics of keeping quiet for the sake of harmony and keeping peace in an environment to raise your children. Perhaps you are living off the unconditional love from your children to balance the pain of a marriage lacking intimacy, while giving up on trusting God for change.

These may be some thoughts that have stolen your ability to trust God for a healed marriage.

1. God won't be able to heal my husband for the sake of our intimacy because my husband's pain is too deep. He doesn't want to deal with it, or he doesn't know how to deal with it, or he is afraid of knowing the truth when the lid is off his pain.

2. I don't want to rock the boat with my emotional needs because my husband is a good provider.

3. He is a good father to the children and they love him, and this is a gratifying substitute for his lack of passion and intimacy towards me.

4. I am no longer attractive enough to successfully marry again.

5. I'd rather be lonely in my marriage in a nice house with its vacation and retirement package, than to be lonely living in an apartment trying to cover expenses for the care of my children.

For those who consider their emotional future bleak, God has big promises for you. Those who become knowledgeable and wise about God's requirements for wives, learn that God can change a heart! Proverbs 21:1 says, "The king's heart is like channels of water in the hand of the Lord; He turns it wherever he wishes." The king is your husband, the one who oversees his kingdom (his family); and Father God is saying, "And I can turn his heart to obey My truths and seek My face."

To understand what God requires of a wife, focus on just that—being a wife, not a good mother, sister, or daughter. Examine your position as a godly wife and perhaps at the same time, understand the emotional baggage that you also brought into the marriage, and its negative influences.

We know that when the husband is healed, the wife is automatically healed. In the meantime, while waiting for that marvelous day—we can work on us.

Helper—The Wife's Rule

The Scripture reference for this rule is Genesis 2:18, "Then the Lord God said, It is not good for the man to be alone; I will make him a helper suitable for him."

What do you think God had in mind? Father God knew exactly what He was planning. All of the animals, fish, and birds had mates "suitable" to their species. Adam, who was made in God's image, needed a suitable mate. Not identical, but suitable. God called that suitable mate *helper*. Understanding what is and is not required of a helper, is a way to clarify blurred boundary lines in our marriage.

Webster's Dictionary defines helper:

> Help (noun): aid, assistance; a source of aid; remedy, relief; one who assists another.

> Helpmate (noun): helper; wife.

For example, the wife (helper) is asked by her husband to pay the bills each month and mail them. She shouldn't be asked by the husband to bring in the money to pay the bills, nor is she required to juggle the money around to pay the bills. That is not her responsibility. As a helper, the wife helps. She does not enable. When a wife enables her husband, she then allows him that right of passage, every time, to hold her responsible for paying the bills.

The helper gets her marching orders from the boss—her husband. In the early years of marriage, those details are usually worked out so each spouse knows what is required of them, right? Why then the confusion of roles and boundaries in marriage? Marriage can't be called a joint venture when both spouses do the same job. Success comes when each partner operates in his or her expertise, thus bringing balance and fulfillment to the venture. Knowing well your position as helper will clarify confusion and hurt feelings in the marriage and bring the harmony that both spouses desire.

We wives naturally want to help our guys and not let them get too overwhelmed with the day-to-day pressures of running a home and keeping a marriage alive. I want to be very clear on this point—this is not your job—as a helper. Allowing them to become overwhelmed may be part of God's plan to get their attention for change. Let's not step in front of God.

As you come alongside your husband and inquire what he needs you to do, this re-enforces several things in your marriage. He will be ever mindful that you hold him totally responsible to make wise decisions for you and the family. However, if you continue to make choices for him, he will either kick back and let you "run the show" (as you wonder why you are always tired and lacking his support); or, he may choose not to share details with you and make the decisions on his own.

Wives, I know what you are thinking, "My husband is too slow in follow-up or he makes mistakes because he doesn't look at all the consequences in his decision making." It is still not your job to step in front of your husband and handle his responsibilities. Perhaps you consider him an immature husband that never grew up. And perhaps this is true. What would be your next step to take, as his helper? After all, you did say, "Yes" when he proposed and you married him.

Most husbands who are still immature do not call their childish actions by this name. They only know that they are unsure of their responsibilities as a husband because they don't understand why they feel ill equipped to make those mature, manly decisions, or how to relate to their wives in manly ways. So to over-compensate for this short fall, the husband will "parent" his wife and in return, the wife will "mother" her husband. Consequently, they both get confused, as to who really is in charge of their marriage.

Obviously, mothering keeps him a child, as he watches for your applause and approval. When one partner stops dancing, the "room-mate dance" stops. Stop mothering and step back. His reaction may surprise you. He may realize that something is very wrong in the marriage. He may even ask you. Be honest with your answers because he truly doesn't know.

Husbands who have not been drawn to their full manhood by their earthly fathers cannot be drawn out to manhood by their wife. This never works. Wives don't have the authority for this responsibility. I tried every combination of solutions and approaches to help my husband. After the rejections, the crying, and the blaming, I finally moved aside for God to step in front of me and take over. By the way, I discovered a truth in this process. If my life gets choppy, irritated, or frustrated, I've stepped in front of God, but when I am walking behind Him, life is manageable. I might add, that for whatever reason, God is often a slow walker.

That tendency to step in front of God for the sake of helping my husband had to go to the cross with the correct name attached. With me, it was co-dependency, gaining my worth by meeting someone else's needs. Helping my husband by handling his responsibilities made me indispensable, and gave me the "strokes of self-worth" I thought I needed to validate my existence.

This self-examination and its discovery did not come overnight, and its deliverance was even further off. But I was on a hunt for freedom. I knew that God had all the answers if I was willing to be honest with the unmet needs behind my motives and actions in my marriage. My heart "ouched" with an anguishing cry when Father God showed me my co-dependency. He explained to me that Jesus was not co-dependent. Jesus let Peter deny Him three times, Jesus didn't chase after Peter to keep him in check. Jesus allowed the consequences of Peter's actions to take place. I finally realized how I was hindering God's work in my husband's life by my lack of knowledge on how to be a godly helper. This co-dependency revealed to me my charade of helping my husband while nurturing my own feelings of self-worth.

With the ability to see the lack of manhood in your husband comes the solution—*prayer*. Yes, it's time consuming—probably quicker just to do it yourself—is your thought. Wrong, unless you plan on mothering your husband indefinitely, the shorter route is prayer. Praying the Word of God sure gets God's attention to oversee its fulfillment, along with sending His angels out to perform it.

After we have been honest about our motives for mothering our husband, who hasn't fully matured into manhood, let's get those motives to the cross. Perhaps you had to perform for love and validation growing up. Then forgive your parents for withholding unconditional love. Perhaps your parents were raised that way themselves. Be kind to your parents and forgive their lack of intimate nurture. Most parents love their children deeply. However, it's the lack of an outward loving expression that confuses the child and leaves them emotionally empty.

Joy's Story

As the eldest of four daughters, with the first three born within twenty-eight months, I became my Mom's assistant. I knew my Mom loved me deeply, but I never got the cuddling and kisses when tucked in bed. I was the one helping my Mom with my sisters at bedtime and then put myself to bed. So I learned early how to perform for my Mother's approval and attention.

This spilled over into my marriage as I attempted to get my husband's attention, approval, and love. Frustration marked each of my efforts to draw my husband out to validate my womanhood. I kept my head down as I raced against all his subtle rejections. Then, I realized I was emotionally empty and so was Michael.

Bombarding my loving Father God with endless prayers for help and wisdom, He revealed to me my co-dependency. I read every book printed on the subject until I got my deliverance to stop this painful fruitless cycle in my life. I moved slowly so I wouldn't be tempted to put back on those familiar co-dependent shoes. Each day I found myself crying and hating myself for all the manipulation and emotional mind games I played when challenged with the appropriate response to my husband. It was a two-year, everyday process. I wanted to be free of performing for love. And my freedom did come and those old familiar shoes—lost their charm.

Shortly after this, Father God gave me a very special gift. I was serving on a Christian woman's weekend (Tres Dias). At bedtime, in a darkened room of twenty-two women sleeping in buck beds, I found my way to my bed on the top bunk. Stretching out and positioning myself so as not to roll off this twin size bed-in-the-air made me a little anxious. My eyes were closed for less then a few minutes when I *saw* the Lord looking down at me as He leaned over to lift my upper body into His arms. He softly said to me, "I want to give you the love you never got from your mother." I could *feel* His love filling my heart. The feeling of this validation intoxicated me. I drifted off into a very deep, healing sleep.

I tested myself the next time I was around my wonderful Mom and found that, indeed, I was free from performance and that I could embrace my Mom with genuine feelings of love. How sweet was this freedom? It was beyond my imagination, and I have a highly skilled imagination.

If you are struggling with performing for love, this prayer may be helpful. It is not a one-time prayer. The travel time between head and heart varies with each individual. It's only when the prayer comes from the heart that there is freedom and deliverance. Don't quit—the freedom is sweet. This freedom will also neutralize the pain of rejection when dealing with your husband's lack of passion.

The Prayer

I forgive you Mom and/or Dad for your lack of loving validation in my life growing up. I forgive you for the feelings of rejection I felt when hoping to get your love and approval. I forgive you for my poor self-image and my lack of self-confidence due to your lack of nurturing. And Father God, I ask in the name of Jesus, that you forgive my parents for their lack of love and validation over my life. Amen.

To your inner child:

To my precious loveable <u>(insert your name)</u>, forgive me for demanding perfection from you and not loving you the way I should. Forgive me for ignoring your needs for the sake of others. You are precious in my sight, and I love you.

Father God, as the loving "parent" that you are, I ask in the name of Jesus, that you would re-parent me and fill my heart full of the love I never received from my parents. Allow me to be a vessel of honor in your eyes. Let my life please you, always. Amen.

When the veil is lifted from your eyes, you see the dance of performing for love (which has been my favorite two-step) finally stopped. Perhaps as your husband sees a change in your demeanor, he would also be interested in this prayer. Please do not feed this prayer to him unless requested, so that he may be won without a word, observing your chaste and respectful behavior. Silence has a loud victory sound.

Being a helper is an honorable position. God not only designed us to be the helper, but He equipped us. According to scientific findings on infants' development, God has made the female's right brain *and* left brain for the purpose of multi-tasking. This frustrates most men's concept of logic, because God designed the male's right brain *or* left brain for the purpose of focus. How helpful that we are designed to multi-task, for cooking, helping with homework, folding clothes, and talking on the phone—all at the same time. A wise husband respects these male-female differences and lets his wife "do her thing" without making her feel "doing his thing" brings love and approval.

Companion—The Wife's Rule

What does the word *companion* imply? Does His Word qualify for the female gender only? Or does it refer to both genders?

Webster's Dictionary defines:

> Companion is an intimate friend or associate—one who is closely connected with something similar.

> Compatible (adjective): able to exist or act together harmoniously

There is nowhere in the Word of God, that I have found, where the wife is referred to as a companion to her husband. God refers to the wife as a "suitable helper," He states this twice in:

Genesis 2:18: "I will make him a helper suitable for him."

Genesis 2:20: "For Adam there was not found a helper suitable for him."

A companion, by definition, is one who is closely connected with something similar. I think Adam's rib qualifies for *connected with something similar*, therefore, making Eve his wife—his companion.

The wife is not just a helper, but also a suitable helper, a companion to her husband. I have often wondered why God seemed more concerned about the man being alone then the woman. I believe men need fellowship with another part of himself by which he can understand his life's purpose. Just as Father God, desires fellowship and made us in His image, He gave men a suitable mate. Alike but different, same but different which gives the difference between spouses its wholeness. A wife to fulfill her God given position in the marriage, she is not called to be just a helper but a suitable-helper and therefore a companion to her husband.

Did you know you are a suitable-helper—designed by God for His purpose in your marriage? Some may be too hurt to be their husband's companion, but they don't mind being his helper. So, let's pray ladies. Let's pray for a healed heart and healed memories. Once we accomplish this healing with our parents, issues with our husbands will belong to him totally. Remember, only your husband can pray his "stuff" to the Cross—you are powerless to make his confessions to God for him. Therefore, let's pray for our guys and trust God with the results.

Intimacy—The Wife's Rule

To wives, intimacy either evokes a feeling of a warm, soft blanket around your heart or a cold shoulder. Either way, intimacy is very important in validating your womanhood. Intimacy defines your sexuality. Intimacy keeps your heart hopeful during tough challenging times. And the absence of passionate intimacy can convince you that you are not desirable or worthy.

You probably wonder why I listed intimacy as one of the rules for the wife. I did because God assigned this to the wife—to desire intimacy. Genesis 3:16 says, "and your desire shall be for your husband."

In most cases, wives are looking for intimacy that isn't necessarily packaged around sex. Husbands may get a little confused here, but they can understand when they are not meeting your intimate needs. The solution is what eludes them.

Webster's Dictionary defines:

> Intimate/intimacy: marked by a very close association, contact, familiarity; marked by a warm friendship; informal warmth or privacy; a very personal or private nature.

> Passion: strong feelings; love; an object of affection or enthusiasm, sexual desire.

Would it be fair to say that wives look for "a passion" from their husband, with whom they desire to be intimate? Disappointed that the passion never came? Disappointed that it was "just sex" and not intimacy? Unfortunately, desire for your husband will continue to burn. Do husbands not know they have this captive audience when they marry? Is this really fair?

Some of these questions were woven into my prayers, as I looked for answers. While driving and chit chatting with the Lord one day, I began to remind Him of things Michael would continually do that hurt me. Michael's responses so often appeared insensitive. Then the Lord spoke quite firmly to my spirit, "Joy, why do you keep tattling on your husband? Don't you know that Satan tattles on the saints all day long?" That hurt. He continued, "Why don't you just ask me what you want?" God got my attention that day and changed my prayers from praying *about* my husband to praying *for* my husband.

We are designed by God to desire intimacy with our husbands. Some believe it's for the benefit of childbirth. When God told Eve that, "in pain she would bear children," God quickly followed by, "and your desire shall be for your husband." This could have some merit. Desire would definitely help in the motivation toward sex for the sake of having children. God is also into intimacy that is fueled by desire. Otherwise, God would not have to command the husband, four times in His Word, "and you shall cleave [have a passion, desiring] to your wife."

And in Song of Solomon 7:10, "I am my beloved's, And his desire is for me."

Our God desires our passion and intimacy. This is also a snapshot of how our relationship with Him should look. Thus, He establishes the model of a marriage with this same picture of passionate intimacy in mind.

How does the desire He creates in wives work into His plans? Could it be that otherwise, husbands would only want sex and not a full expression of love? Or is the husband's struggle in his intimacy with Father God, also a reflection of the struggles in his intimacy with his wife?

In the quest for answers to marital loneliness, wives may find it easy to lay blame on the husband's inability to bring passion into the sexual arena. This may be true, but careless, hurtful execution of this truth can bring resentment or cause the husband's hearing to fail. We need God's wisdom here. Being right doesn't mean we win.

A husband knows his role is to bring passion into his marriage (cleave) and to role model intimacy (lover). A husband who fails in this area of passionate lover often struggles from early childhood issues that hinder him from fulfilling successfully his wife's desires. Only he can work on that. Only he can say the prayers needed for deliverance. Only he can say, "I need help." Such husbands need us to give them room to work it out with God.

That is not to say, act like a robot wife. Your feelings and need for intimacy are important and should be expressed to your husband in a language he understands. Usually this is not when you are on your last straw or tired. Once you have stated clearly and kindly how your needs for intimacy from him are not being met, then stand back. God heard you, even if your husband didn't.

The revelation knowledge in His Word and its anointing will deliver freedom to the coldest roommate marriage and is available to all that believe in Him. Trust God to deliver on His Word.

A lovely lady friend of mine, a successful Christian counselor, who knew I was writing this book on marriage, asked me if there was recourse for a woman whose husband doesn't cleave and has no desire to seek counsel? I was challenged by this question and took it to God for His answer. And answer me, He did. The moment the question was off my lips, "What is a wife to do in a marriage where the husband doesn't cleave and doesn't care to change? Do You leave these wives stranded in these cold marriages?"

I immediately saw, in a vision, Christ standing very tall behind a husband and in front of the husband, his wife is kneeling at Christ's feet praying. I inquired as to its translation and the Lord said, "I am the head of the husband, the wife is praying to Me, and putting Me in remembrance of My Word, as it regards her husband. I am changing the course of the husband's heart." That's the answer. A wife's scriptural prayer will allow God to change a husband's heart to embrace His perfect plan for their marriage.

Proverb 21:1 says, "The king's [husband's] heart is in My [God's] hands as streams of water that I [God] can turn to the right or left."

Along with this revelation came a full understanding of the power of prayer, according to God's will. As I began to type out a prayer for the wives, the Lord interrupted my thoughts with a reminder of the work He did in my life. This gave Him clear passage to do His work in my husband's heart; more on this later in *Joy's Story*.

The information and prayer for a wife stranded in a roommate marriage is best captured in my email message to my friend:

> Below is the response I got from Father God while lifting up your question to Him:
>
> "What is a wife to do with a husband who doesn't cleave, doesn't want to change, and doesn't want to see a counselor, after she has done everything she can think of to shake him up?"
>
> "God does not leave wives defenseless and incapable of initiating change. First comes change in the wife's behavior coupled with enlisting His help. The wife will have to be diligent to know and use wisely the Word of God because wives see so clearly their husband's issues. As the wife gives these issues to God, she will have a front-row seat as she witnesses the hand of God at work in her marriage. This may take longer than a wife would want to wait. But it's the only sure solution to a permanent change. Most women don't mind waiting nine

months for that sweet, precious, new member of the family to arrive. Our husbands deserve the same patience."

"First, the wife must be about her own baggage, which she brought into the marriage and her husband may not have taken the initiative to remove, either through his lack of understanding Numbers 30 or just lack of wisdom that his wife needs counseling. Either way, she needs to work on her stuff."

"Her stuff smells like this. Every time her husband says or does something that hurts her, this is a flesh pattern that is not dead from her past, because dead flesh doesn't hurt. (The wife will need to use wisdom as to whether this hurt was a judgment from her formative years or judgment from his growing up years.) It took me several years to understand that my particular hurt was from my judgment made in *my* youth."

Joy's Story

After Michael and I were first married, he would look at other women—follow them with his eyes—look them up and down and was not even aware that he was doing it or that it bothered me. But I soon showed my irritation. Whenever it would happen, which was every time we went out, especially to any of the church services or programs. Michael said I was crazy. That he was just looking around at the people and enjoying the socializing.

After two years of this looking at other women, I was becoming very anti-social and preferred to stay at home. This did not solve my problem. Reviewing in my mind, Michael's childhood and his father's behavior, I couldn't connect this behavior of looking at other women to Michael's side of the family. But in reviewing the dynamics between my parents, this situation of looking at other women came into clear focus. (Michael never looked at other women while we were dating or engaged, which later, after we married, kept me guessing as to the source of my frustration and pain with his newly acquired habit.)

I remembered my mother complaining to my father about the same thing year after year. It never stopped. He would constantly look other woman up and down. What I couldn't understand was, why the pain? My mother, being so beautiful, out-shined any woman my father would ever look at, so why did his actions make my mother feel so jealous and insecure?

It took me another year to get to those two words—jealous and insecure—that would finally set me free. This surprised me because I had never been jealous or insecure in any dating relationship in the past. This was a new experience for me.

I had judged my mother's relationship with my father, and had said to myself numerous times, "I'll never be jealous and insecure in my marriage like my mother." How soon I had forgotten that judgment, and the effect this time bomb would have, once I was married. This was indeed, *my issue* and *my problem.* I was reaping this judgment through Michael (See Romans 2:1).

I said my prayer of forgiveness for judging my mother and her marriage. I nailed this judgment to the Cross of Calvary. Relief still did not come.

I would scream this new directive into my heart that "I was not jealous or insecure." For days and weeks on end, I would scream out this new directive with no results.

Then later, I realized that I judged my mother in the midst of her pain. I felt her pain and didn't want any part of it. So I needed to scream this new directive—when in the midst of *my* pain.

I realized if Michael never stopped looking at women, it didn't matter. I just wanted to be free of the nausea of being jealous and insecure. I knew I needed to scream this new directive into my heart—at the time it happened. At the time Michael would be looking at another woman.

Ready with my new game plan, my opportunity for deliverance arrived at a wedding in a small town in north Georgia. As we were standing in the receiving line, Michael started looking up and down at the woman standing in front of us. I excused myself to the ladies room and ran into the small stall, which had been painted too many times with a thick, lumpy red paint color that had blistered over the many coats of years past. (It is amazing what a mind remembers, what the eyes gaze upon, when one is screaming into one's hands in a loud whisper.)

I quickly put both hands over my mouth so that as I screamed this new directive into my heart, I wouldn't alarm the women in the ladies room. I screamed into my hands, "Those feelings of jealousy and insecurity do not belong to me. Those are *not* my feelings. I fall out of agreement with those feelings." (I had to tell my heart in a strong firm manner; this is the truth I choose to embrace.) Immediately, something lifted off me, and *I was free*! I was able to rejoin Michael and enjoy the balance of the wedding celebration.

A week later, as Michael and I were walking through Macy's Department store, his head began to turn to look at a woman on the next aisle. Michael quickly realized what he was doing and said, "I am looking at other women" (which by this time, it didn't bother me). Michael took authority over his action and nailed it to the Cross. And that was the end of that. My judgment defiled Michael and when I got free, Michael was able to *see* it and be free.

Without the quest for truth, the revelation, taking the sin of judgment to the cross, and destroying false directives to my heart, my jealousy and insecurity would continue to eat at the foundation of our marriage until either our marriage or I were destroyed. Time would never be able to negate the power and authority this judgment held over our marriage relationship. This judgment would last for the duration of my marriage until it was dealt with and destroyed. Honesty, in calling out your pain by the right name, will always bring deliverance.

Each wife should prayerfully reflect on issues about her husband that irritate her and be careful to rightly discern to whom those issues fall. Only the wife can do her prayer work because only she made the judgment with her heart.

Second

These are the four things that Father God showed me that a wife can do when her husband does not cleave or does not desire to change.

Only Father God can change the husband's heart. Remember, Jesus is the husband's head and He has the authority to feed new information into the husband's heart.

A Wife's Position with Her Husband

1. Forgive him daily for rejecting you emotionally.

- Lack of passion
- Not validating your womanhood
- Not feeling safe and secure
- For the loneliness

2. Remind God of His Word

Examples:

> For I am watching over My word to perform it.
> —JEREMIAH 1:12

> Put me in remembrance [of my word], let us argue our case together; State your cause, that you may be proved right.
> —ISAIAH 43:26

> Bless the Lord, you His angels, mighty in strength, who perform His word, obeying the voice of His word."
> —PSALM 103:20

Remind God of His Scripture that reflects your rights as a wife. There are three verses that are strong anchors in a marriage for a wife along with its promises that are in line with God's will.

> For this reason a man shall leave his father and mother, and be joined [cleave] to his wife and the two shall become one flesh.
> —1 MATTHEW 19:5

Husbands love your wives—nourish and cherish her as Christ loved the church.

—EPHESIANS 5:25, 29 (AUTHOR'S PARAPHRASE)

You Husbands in the same way, live with your wives in an understanding way, as with someone weaker, since she is a woman; and show her honor as a fellow heir of the grace of life, so that your prayers may not be hindered."

—1 PETER 3:7

Daily, lift these scriptures to God and put Him in remembrance.

3. A wife's prayer

Most Gracious and Holy Father God, Your Word brings life and freedom to the captives. You say, Father God, to put You in remembrance of Your Word and to state my case. You also say that You oversee Your Word to perform it. With that being said, Most Gracious and Holy Father God, I petition you in the name of Jesus to oversee and grant my verbal request.

That my husband, (insert your husband's name), would leave his father and mother, emotionally and with forgiveness, and that my husband, (insert your husband's name), would cleave intimately to me in oneness with a deep, abiding love of passion. To nourish and cherish me intimately and to live with me in an understanding way, with knowledge, knowing that I am a weaker vessel with physical and emotional limitations—along with showing me respect and protection because I am a woman. Amen.

This may need to be a daily prayer until there is a break through in his behavior, which may even run the length of the marriage. The advantage is God's Word does not return void.

You are giving God the request of what is rightfully yours, as He planned. This prayer does not tell God where to work on your husband. It is a powerful prayer because you are leaving all the work and details up to God.

4. Break Agreements made with your mouth, to yourself, to your spouse, or to relatives and friends.

> *I break my agreement with my husband that we will always struggle emotionally, sexually, _____,*
> *_____, _____. I break my agreement with my mother, father, sisters, brothers, and friends that I married a _____ (loser, unkind, unloving, self-centered, etc.) man. I break my agreement with all my negative confessions that I spoke in reference to my husband (list them) _____, _____,*
> *_____, _____.*

> **Break Judgments** *you made about your father's actions in his marriage.*

> *Father God, I ask in Jesus' name for your forgiveness for all the many times I judged my father's actions and*

demeanor in his marriage to my mother. Forgive me for judging my father and saying _____,

_____, _____ *(i.e., I will never marry a man like my father, I'll never marry a man who has a temper like my father, I'll never marry a man who makes me as unhappy as he has made my mother, etc.)*

And/Or

I'll never be in a marriage like my mother's, with a husband who is _____, _____,

_____ *(i.e., unkind, easily irritated, unloving, rude, dishonoring, selfish, etc.).*

"I ask, Father God, that You would void and destroy all those judgments and vows I made in my heart. Judgments I made against my mother, father, and husband. In nailing them to the Cross of Calvary, I render those judgments and vows dead and inoperative in my life and in my marriage, in Jesus' name." Amen.

"Most Holy Father God I ask for Your forgiving mercy towards me, to cancel the consequences that I would reap for all the judgments I made of my father's and mother's behavior in their marriage. I ask this in Jesus' name." Amen.

This prayer about judging your father is an on-going prayer until positive counter-claims drop into your heart and destroy the lies you believed about men. There is no short cut, just a straight route to freedom. You will know when you are free. God does not leave wives in hopeless marriages. Prove God in this. And if you need to leave, He will show you the way.

These prayers were given to a wife who allowed me insight into the challenges in her marriage. Without knowledge of her prayers, her husband's demeanor and actions toward her began to change. She would e-mail joyful news about changes in his demeanor toward her. Here are her early e-mails to bring encouragement to us all.

She was given the above prayers in late April.

1. **Email #1, July 14:** "Your prayer is being heard by the Big Man (God), and my husband is responding with a softened heart towards me—great results; and especially how he is starting to become more protective over me, which never before crossed his mind. Thank you."

2. **Email #2, August 9:** "I did want you to know that my husband has taken on a peculiar but very likable attitude towards me of protection that I have never seen before. Also, the prayer is being read in the a.m. with his Bible study times. He also has mentioned so many times with our "housing" situation that it is up to him to take care of us and that he needs to do something about it. Of course I let him, and I think that

this is big too, that I am releasing my control to him. We are making baby steps every day because of your powerful prayer and how the Lord has lead you— thank you so much."

3. **Email #3, August 28:** "My husband is following a different path with his attitude, and I am so grateful for the Lord and His infinite wisdom and *prayers*!!! I just had my prayer time, and everyday your prayer is amazing me with growth from my partner as we cling to each other in these tumultuous times."

4. **Email #4, September 9:** "I hope you are smiling because once again we are feeling, sensing, and praying your prayers with commitment and reso- lution. This past Sunday, my husband and I looked at each other and forgave one another for all that had transpired in the past—how releasing. We are re-committing ourselves to one another."

When everything else fails, prayer works. Most often our frustra- tion with prayer is that we want it to change our husbands and whip them into line. I am sure Father God has had some good laughs with my efforts in the name of love to change my husband. Let us be wise and charming. You know that God made women charming, don't you?

Husbands in roommate marriages, who are blocked from cleaving with passionate intimacy to their wives, may not know they often become high maintenance husbands—emotionally and physically. They may appear self-centered, self-focused, easily irritated, and non-protective of the physical limitations of their wives. When the wife acts like that's OK behavior, the husband does not think he is doing anything wrong. The frustration is the balance in letting him know its *not* OK behavior, especially if you are raising young male children, who will reflect their father's behavior when they marry.

> The glory of sons is their father.
> —PROVERBS 17:6

Praying before speaking to our husbands helps us communicate clearly. Honesty always brings freedom when shared in the spirit of love. Sometimes silence is not golden.

Wives in these roommate marriages who have sons should guard filling their emotional void by drawing one of their sons into meeting their needs, whether on a conscious or subconscious level. Most male children are clueless to these unspoken demands and accommodate their mother's wishes of *notice me, compliment me, give me attention,* and so on. It really needs to stop! This affects the son's ability to have a balanced and cleaving relationship with his future wife. If your husband doesn't cleave to you, it is often because of something his mother did or didn't do to him in his formative years. Let us not repeat this cycle. This can stop with our generation.

Guard your behavior around your sons and keep the mother-son relationship in its correct balance. Be a grateful mother, not a *needy* woman. Your husband may never cleave and be intimate with you. Your choices are the prayers listed above, counseling, or a separation to work on your marriage. The dynamics between you and your husband do not fool your children. So let God work on your marriage. You have nothing to lose and everything to gain—like a new husband, who is as charming as the first time he caught your eye. It's worth the effort.

For the benefit of marriage counselors reading this book, wives in roommate marriages will do any one of the following to counterbalance their lack of intimacy and validation:

- Get their love and validation through a son and/or grandson.

If the children are all females, or there are no children, the wives seem to favor these choices:

- Stay busy with activities at the church or a ministry or a "cause."

- Start a career to get the approval, the recognition, the validation, or monies to escape.

- Investing in other people lives—feeling needed.

- Over-eating comfort foods, looking fat (could also keep a husband at a distance).

- Take prescription drugs to numb the loneliness.

- Have an affair or affairs (especially if her sexual boundary was violated growing up).

- Get a separation.

- Get a divorce.

Peace comes only when we do it God's way. Let us not be destroyed for the lack of His knowledge. I am mindful that I wake up every day in the flesh and thus begin the struggles. But our will should be stronger than our flesh and, therefore, carry us over to victory to do it God's way. Even when we mess up, He is there to see us through.

Loneliness is a cold companion, which leaves desperation in the hearts of so many wives in roommate marriages. Honesty will always take you to freedom. Evaluate your relationship with your husband and set your course to victory. Father God is intimately aware of every detail of your marriage. Nothing you share with Him will come as a surprise although His response to you may bring surprising revelations. Be kind to yourself. You are beautiful, charming, and deserving of a passionate romance.

Subject to Husband's Authority—The Wife's Rule

How often, when we women hear the word *"submission,"* does something gripping and controlling seem to slip around our necks and cause anxiety to come over us? Is your heart racing a little faster? Don't worry. God's definition of *submit* brings with it protection, responsibility, and tender care.

Wives need to understand clearly the order of headship that Father God has set up. He is the head of Jesus Christ and Jesus does only what He sees the Father do. God is Jesus' authority, and Jesus submits to Him. Jesus Christ is the head of the husband and the husband should submit to Jesus and do what he *sees* Jesus do. Next, the husband is head of the wife and she should submit to her husband and do what she *sees* her husband do.

When husbands don't submit to God's commands, it's hard for wives to submit to the husband's commands. Where is the fairness in this? What could God possibly be thinking when He laid this *submission* on the wife?

Let's return to the Garden of Eden where it all started.

Genesis, chapters 2 and 3, tell the story of the perfect couple, Adam and Eve, passionately in love, walking quietly through a perfect, well-manicured garden with breathtaking flowers and foliage lining its borders and hugging the base of luscious fruit trees. The atmosphere is laced with all the wonderful smells of sun-ripe fruit and fragrant flowers in full bloom. Everything is in order, under a canopy of peace. Can you feel the serenity?

This is the sequence of events that changed their serenity:

1. God gives Adam a direct command *not* to eat of the tree of the knowledge of good and evil in the middle of the Garden.

2. Adam gives Eve the command not to eat of the tree in the middle of the Garden.

3. Satan is tempting Eve to be disobedient to her husband, Adam, by eating the forbidden fruit from the tree in the middle of the garden

4. Eve takes the fruit off the tree and eats it—nothing happened.

5. Eve gives the fruit to Adam, who is with her.

6. Adam eats the fruit and then *both* their eyes are opened.

Adam disobeys God and Eve disobeys Adam. God then banishes Adam and Eve from His paradise garden and they are escorted out of the Garden of Eden. This leaves Adam to toil in the hard barren soil for their survival and Eve with birth pains to bring forth children after their own likeness ("and the two shall become one flesh").

So whose fault is it that this happened? The travesty is they are both to blame, though the responsibility for this error in judgment falls totally to Adam. Adam did not protect his wife from eating of the tree of knowledge of good and evil even though Eve disobeyed her husband's command. Because the authority from God was given to Adam, this tells us why both Adam and Eve's eyes did not open until *after* Adam ate the forbidden fruit.

Adam decisions carry with it his authority of control over his environment.

Unknowingly, Eve influenced the very person, Adam, who was unaware of his authority over his life and his wife's. Then, as Adam doubted and questioned the validity of God's command not to eat of the forbidden fruit, he chose to be disobedient with his wife, Eve. Adam's disobedience brought about irreversible consequences that would change their resident address—forever.

Thus, Father God gave a command to Eve, "and he (Adam) shall rule over you." Therefore, Adam would be accountable to God for the use of his authority in the care and safety of his wife. The husband is to keep his wife out of harms way; to keep her safe from the lies of the enemy and protect her from wrong decisions. The husband is to rule with protection over his wife, take care of her, provide for her, and keep her safe. This is a wonderful picture of a secure and stable marriage.

To wives in roommate marriages, why is this protection not working? You don't like the way your husband asks, commands, and scolds you to submit? You feel you make better decisions than he? He doesn't obey God, so why should you obey his voice? God has given him authority with *his* mouth, whether he knows it or not. Whether he uses it for good or for evil, the authority still stands. So let's not provoke him and bring harsh, negative words out of his mouth and over your life.

The solution for such conflicts of authority and submission is found in the Word of God. When my late husband, Michael, made a decision with which I did not agree, I would say, "I don't agree." Our family decisions were only made after we talked it out and were in agreement. When a wife simply says, "I don't agree," you get their attention. (This approach of resolving conflict came about after several years of stand-off disagreements.)

After all, God so designed it that man should not be alone. What husband would want to walk down the street of his decision alone? It may take two "I disagrees" to change his decision. Your husband needs and values your support. A wise husband understands the power of agreement. Matthew 18:19 says, "Again I say to you, that if two of you agree on earth about anything that they may ask, it shall be done for them by My Father who is in heaven."

However, when you say, "I disagree," don't badger your husband into changing his mind. Those changes or compromises need to be his decision. Otherwise, you risk becoming controlling and could evoke being called that name often by his mouth. The journey back to his renouncing this name he spoke over you may take more time than you had to give it, in addition to undoing the character change it made in you.

There is comfort and a sense of protection when a husband is in charge, especially when he uses his voice and words to bless our life. That's the perfect picture. But what if it doesn't work that way in your home? Some husbands are lazy, lack follow-through, can't make a decision, makes poor decisions, or are commanding and demanding. What is a wife to do? These are the choices God gives us:

> Submit yourself for the Lord's sake to every human institu-
> tion, whether to a king as the one in authority [husband], or
> to the government [that rules over your life].
>
> —1 Peter 2:13

> Honor all men; love the brotherhood, fear God, honor the
> king [husband].
>
> —1 Peter 2:17

We are to submit to our husband's authority because God put him in charge of our life to watch over our safety. We are to be mindful of the position of authority that our husbands hold. I have lived this concept a long time before, *I got it*: "submit to your husband, be subject to your husband, and be obedient to your husband."

> For this finds favor, if for the sake of conscience toward God,
> a person [a wife] bears up under sorrows when suffering
> unjustly.
>
> —1 Peter 2:19

In the same way, you wives, be submissive to your own husbands so that even if any of them are disobedient to the word, they may be won without a_word by the behavior of their wives.

—1 PETER 3:1, EMPHASIS ADDED

Father God requires we wives to be respectful of our husband's place of authority over us, because in doing so, we honor God and His purpose in our lives. Father God will not require something of us that He has not first equipped us to fulfill. As a woman and a wife, He has so designed us to become dependent on our husband's authority. When wives lose this focus, the marriage becomes a tug of war. It's hard for God to live and reside in a house of chaos. When one partner changes, the dance stops! Mark out *your* boundaries, ladies, and stay on your side of the line!

Do you want to find favor with God? You will have to live according to His *rules* and not what you consider "fair." Of course, this does not mean staying in a physically or mentally abusive marriage. First Peter 3:6 states, "Just as Sarah obeyed Abraham, calling him lord, and you have become her children if you do what is right without being frightened by any fear." If you are fearful for your well-being, and safety, and that of your children, by all means protect yourself and seek refuge in a safe place. Get godly counsel on the next step to take.

For wives living in a roommate marriage, God has equipped us to bring our marriage in line with His will by our chaste, obedient behavior. He requires this of us, because He gave us our desire for someone in authority over our life, to be responsible for our well-being, safety, and happiness.

Let's remind ourselves of the vow we made before God, when we agreed to marry our husband—for good or bad. We were not forced to marry this man, and if we failed to do a thorough check-up on his abilities as husband and father, this still does not negate the contract you made before God to respect his position of authority.

Your husband is required by God and is accountable to God for your well-being, whether he is aware of it or not. Your *rule* is to obey and be mindful of what is required of you in your position as wife. Keeping score of your husband's failures is too time consuming and unproductive. Let's be about our own stuff.

Plan a meeting with your husband, so you can understand what he requires of you and the support he needs from you. Most husbands want to be their wife's hero. Coming home to a woman with her arms crossed, tapping her foot is a bad way to end his day. Remember, God made His women charming, clever, and smart.

> She opens her mouth in wisdom, and the teaching of kindness is on her tongue.
> —PROVERBS 31:26

The last part of scripture in 1 Peter 3:1, "they [husbands] may be won without a word by the behavior of their wives," can often redirect a husband's next move when he is disobedience. Silence can be that provocative visitor in the room—a quiet spirit gets. Proverbs 17:28 says, "Even a fool, when he keeps silent, is considered wise; when he closes his lips, he is counted prudent."

A prayer can help:

> *Father God, in the name of the Lord Jesus Christ,*
> *my savior and Lord, I ask for Your peace and favor*
> *as I respond respectfully to my husband's authority.*
> *Grant my husband, _____, wisdom and*
> *favor in everything to which he lays his hand. That*
> *You would teach him in the way he should go and*
> *show him how to use his authority for Your glory. I ask*
> *that my husband, _____, would live with*
> *me according to godly knowledge, and with this, bring*
> *Christ-like harmony and behavior to our relation-*
> *ship. Grant my husband success as he applies Your*
> *"rules" and "roles" to his life and our marriage. Grant*
> *me wisdom on when to be silent and when to speak.*
> *Give me patience to allow You ample room and time*
> *to work in our marriage and to work in my heart. It is*
> *in your Holy name, Lord Jesus, I ask this. Amen.*

This could be your *daily* prayer for a season, giving God permission to work in your heart and your husband's. Only God can change a heart. Only God can convict with permanent repentance. God is seeking hearts that need Him. Lay aside your program of defense, or program of survival, and let God fight your battles in your marriage. Need I remind you of God's majesty in how He turned the enemies on themselves in battle in those suspense-gripping stories of the Old Testament? God sees and knows *everything* about your marriage. He is waiting to be invited in.

Some wives become "robotic obedient wives" to survive. This is not pleasing to God, because it does not allow Him access to work in your husband's heart. Many husbands fail to understand the finite details of the problems in their roommate marriage, which usually is focused on meeting their needs first. A wife's action when helping her husband, accomplish *his rules and roles*, especially in the area of money, may seem obedient, but God reads our heart, knowing the consequences of stepping over boundary lines. Consequently, it can breed rebellion in our heart as we submit to our husband's intimidating tactics of helping him with his duties and responsibilities. If it is not possible to address a husband with legitimate complaints and fears, write a note and pray. God will handle the rest.

Our husbands may be clueless that we are silently disagreeing. Denial is a great comfort when there is fear, argument, or intimidation. At times we must be brave in making a simple request. Men are not skilled mind readers, and perhaps they have become accustomed to our occasional "snippy" remarks, misreading them as "wrong time of the month" talk. Be clear in your communication with them, even if a husband says his wife is "stupid or acting out of line with Scripture." God knows when to pull the plug on all that. "Do not be deceived, God is not mocked; for whatever a man sows, this he will also reap" (Gal. 6:7). Simply trust God. He knows the Word better than your husband and will hold him accountable for every careless word spoken out of balance with His Word. (See Matthew 12:36–37.)

Some outspoken wives find it difficult bearing up under a burden of injustice in their marriage. That is a hardship when trying to understand why God would allow this. However, wives running interference with God prolong the process for successful permanent changes. Remember, God can change your husband's heart to become that protector of your soul and spirit. He just requires our obedience to His Word.

If you are not making headway with your marital issues, why not try it God's way? He sees and knows everything in your heart and your husband's. "Sand bagging" God with self-righteous actions will only bring frustrated results. Let's re-group, change our attitude, and enjoy the challenge of the quest that is at hand in your marriage. His way brings peace, harmony, and unity.

Armed with the knowledge of His Word and a game plan of His strategies in place, the final step is to tie it all up with your "wrapping of charm." Husbands can be charmed by our need for them, which, by the way, is their secret password, *need*. They need to feel needed and important in your life. Proverbs 15:30 says, "Bright eyes gladden the heart; good news puts fat on the bones." Do your eyes light up when you see your husband walking through the door, looking for your warm, approving smile? He could sure use that encouragement.

Gently state the challenges in your marriage in a communication style with your husband that will evoke a positive, constructive response. Use your secret weapon of flattering charm to win over your lost "heart-throb." You are highly skilled at this, you know, with just a wink of the eye. And give him an honest reflection of unresolved issues that need his attention and wisdom. He may not understand in what fashion he is needed to bring you peace.

Chapter II

Roles: Respond, Obey, Respect

Responder—The Wife's Role

WHY DID GOD KNIT this *responder* trait into the psyche of a woman? What was His intention and purpose for this gift? Do women know they have this automatic responder gift? Perhaps it's not thought of as a gift but an irritant. Knowing that God never makes mistakes helps us understand His motivation and purpose for this gift and why this is an automatic role for the wife.

The scripture to support this *gift* is found in:

> But the woman [wife] is the glory of the man [husband].
> —1 CORINTHIANS 11:7

It states throughout the New Testament that, "Jesus glorified the Father." The apostle Paul also stated his purpose was, "to glorify Jesus in all that he does." *Webster's Dictionary* defines *glorify* as "to light up brilliantly." The divine translation for the word *glory* or *glorify* means to "reflect brightly."

1. The woman is to *reflect* the husband's demeanor, actions and attitude shown her—back to him.

2. Jesus *reflects* His Father's demeanor, actions, and attitude to His followers.

3. The Apostle Paul states that he *reflects* Jesus demeanor, actions and attitude in all that he does to the church.

4. As believers, we are to glorify God in our lives. We are to *reflect* His demeanor to those around us.

Wives should ask themselves, "Am I adequately reflecting my husband back to him, consciously or subconsciously?" Why is this important to Father God? It is important for truth, protection, and intimacy. For now, we see in a mirror dimly, but then face-to-face, now I know in part, but then I shall know fully as I also have been fully known. Meaning your husband's reflection is on your face, as if you are holding a mirror in front of your face and your husband *sees* his own reflection. Does your husband like his reflection?

When we look at the expressions on a wife's face, it tells us how well the husband has been doing in the marriage. I am quite sure when the wife is applying her make-up she is not looking at a down-turned mouth or the "puckered lips of bitterness." She sees her face dimly in the mirror's reflection. A candid photograph became my wake-up call—seeing my facial expressions of sadness and hopelessness, which fooled nobody but myself.

God's revelation of this reflection (glory) gift He has bestowed on wives was further explained years later on a Sunday, when a pastor I had never heard preach, spoke about the message he was about to deliver. The title of his message caused me to stop, sit on the ottoman with elbows on my knees and my face in my hands, to drink in every syllable of his message entitled, "Why did God give Adam Eve? To show Adam, Adam." The pastor stated, "What was Eve's job in Paradise? Rake the leaves that hadn't fallen?" He said, "Eve was there by God's design to *reflect* Adam back to Adam. Adam would *see* clearly the effects of his actions—by Eve's reactions and response." Do you think Adam knew? Does your husband know you are reflecting him?

To carry the point this pastor was making about "Eve showing Adam, Adam" a bit further, begs the question, does this give us a different picture of Eve's disobedience in the Garden of Eden? It is something to ponder for sure. Does it have merit? Was Eve merely reflecting Adam's disobedient nature when she disobeyed Adam and ate the forbidden fruit in front of him? After all, Adam was with Eve when she was talking to the serpent? Also Adam was standing next to Eve and watched her eat the forbidden fruit and didn't stop her.

God has made the wife the reflection of the husband by giving her the ability to glorify and reflect her husband back to himself. Some husbands may not like their reflection from their wives, though they are perhaps not in touch with its full significance, when indeed, this *gift* should be a blessing for them. Most often in families, this "reflective revelation" goes undetected until is shows up in their children's behavior.

"The glory of sons is their father" (Prov. 17:6). Another translation states, "the glory of children is their father." While a girl living at home, she reflects her father, but once she marries she reflects her husband's demeanor. The son will always reflect his father's demeanor unless prayers are said by the son to annul that connection, especially if the father is unkind or abusive.

God has given this response-reflective trait to the wife to better steer her husband from harm. After all, Adam said when he first saw Eve, "This is bone of my bones and flesh of my flesh, she shall be called woman, because she was taken out of man" (Gen. 2:23). Eve was, therefore, given the knowledge to *feel* Adam because it was from Adam's cells that Eve was fashioned and made.

Woman originated from live, living organic matter. Thus women were made "touchy and feely" from the beginning of time. Adam was made from inorganic matter, the dust of the earth. Since God did not make Eve from dust, she received this connection of sensing and feeling things about her husband. How marvelous is God in all His planning for intimacy? He left nothing to chance.

If our husbands are disrespectful toward us, it is natural to disrespect him, even when he needs our, applause, approval, and respect. If the husband has been raised in a family that did not show respect, he will become insulated from his parent's rebuke of disrespect as a means of protection. He marries and repeats his parent's abuse of disrespect. As the wife reflects that disrespect, the husband will often respond with criticism. And if you try to explain how disrespectful he is to you, he doesn't *hear* you, because he has insulated himself against your voice of rebuke. This dance can go on for a lifetime. Consequently, if you stop reflecting, truthfully, he begins to lose his way and Satan is applauding.

When God instituted Eve and all women after her to be the "glory of their husbands," to reflect their behavior back to them, it was meant for good. Because Eve was taken from Adam's flesh, Eve therefore would be able to be an honest reflection to keep Adam in check with his behavior. That was God's perfect plan. Then after the fall of Man, these bad and evil choices had the same legal access to the immutable law, of sowing and reaping, which were originally established by God to lavish multiple blessings on mankind; now mankind was able to reap the negative devices of their choices—multiplied.

Yes, God plans for Eve's reflective gift was to show Adam, Adam. This same plan is in force today for wives to reflect their husbands. God did not stop, terminate, eliminate, or destroy any of the immutable laws He instituted, as stated in Genesis chapters one, two, and three. His laws are now operating with the good and the bad, with blessings and curses, with favor and disfavor, until the end of time, when we will have a new heaven and a new earth. In the meantime, let's consider a plan that will promise more good than bad and more passion than loneliness. We can implement this change by "a gentle and quiet spirit, which is precious in the sight of God," (1 Pet. 3:4).

The first requirement for change in the action and reaction between husbands and wives is honesty. This comes first, when we truly intend to adjust our reflection to our husband's actions.

This is what honesty looks like:

1. Have I given my husband the honest reflection/ response to his actions or words toward me?

2. Does he know how lonely and/or unhappy I am in our marriage?

3. Does he know I pretend to be happy to keep peace in our home, for the sake of the children or grandchildren?

These are heavy thought-provoking questions. I know you long to be understood with compassion. Husbands may respond to such questions with feelings of guilt, shame, and/or blame. It will take love and gentle honesty to help your husband understand the consequences of his actions.

Putting your thoughts, fears, and suggestions in writing can help in your honest discussion with your husband. Start with the small stuff and as you build confidence over time, work your way to the big issues. There is no right or wrong technique here, just the truth that will open the door to freedom for both of you. Remember you were given the ability to *read* your husband's *spiritual* DNA and this includes his fears, anxieties, and worries. As you reassure him that you share this journey with him, it brings comfort and helps him fight his demons. A wife's prayers are powerful when lifting up the Word of God and reminding God of the promises He has for your husband and king.

A wife in a roommate marriage needs to define this situation clearly to her husband. Detailed facts are helpful for him to understand the concept and why this loneliness is allowed to operate in your marriage, and what qualifies it to be called a roommate marriage. Husbands usually have a hard time recognizing the roommate marriage syndrome in their marriages and have an even harder time understanding that they are the ones totally responsible for *its* operation.

This issue of responsibility was discussed in detail in the *Cleaving* section of the Husband Section of this book. Your role, as his wife, is to be honest in your responses to him, especially, if your husband asks you to tell him the truth, in a loving, constructive way. He may surprise you with his willingness and his desire to make you happy. After all, you are a significant part of his "report card" before God.

Obedience—The Wife's Role

Some wives panic at the thought of having to obey their husband in everything. But obedience is for our safety and protection. It keeps the focus and pressure on the one in authority in our marriage—our husband. Acting as his helper is a safer, less anxious position, unless a wife opts to take over some of her husband's responsibilities. Then she would feel the stress and pressure that only the husband is physically and emotionally designed by God to handle.

Webster's Dictionary defines:

> Obey: to follow the commands or guidance of; to comply with.

> Obedient: submissive to the restraint or command of authority.

So why is obedience a role for the wife? Why not for the husband also? Because the woman was made for the man and not the other way around, as it states in 1 Corinthians 11:9, "For indeed man was not created for the woman's sake, but the woman for the man's sake." The woman is not the husband's authority or head. She has no anointing of authority from God to support the functioning of his role. It is God's plan and anointing for the husband to take the heat. As God said to Adam, "Cursed is the ground because of you; in toil you shall eat of it all the days of your life" (Gen. 3:17). Would any wife really want to take on this role? Then let your husband lead, and be his obedient helper.

Why does obedience become so confusing? How do these roles get shifted between husband and wife? The lack of God's wisdom, poor role modeling from parents, or disobedience in wanting to do it my-way all lead to poor choices. Knowledge is a powerful ally and holds the answers to these questions.

Obedience is especially hard when you don't respect your husband as a husband or a man, or when he playfully speaks those hurtful jabs over you, which convinces you he considers you a "joke." I have been there, and confess that ultimately my love for God and His rules were greater than issues with my husband. I knew that Father God heard those careless words that were spoken over my life and would handle the outcome of that. More importantly, I didn't want to fall out of favor with God and what He had called me to in my marriage. Hebrews 5:8 states, "He [Jesus] learned obedience from the things which He suffered."

This scripture teaches that obedience is learned and that it's objective, regardless of the person. I had to choose to let God teach me His concept of obedience. I had to press on with great determination to surmount the obstacle of my stubborn disobedience. The closer I got to freedom, the sweeter my voice would sound.

There are several ways to help wives learn their obedience role. The freedom in obeying your husband becomes the fruit of our obedience to the Lord and His perfect will for us as wives. It's simple, though at first it may not seem easy or natural.

Suggested Points of Obedience

1. Be obedient to the words you state, as a confession or agreement.

2. Be obedient to the Word of God.

3. Be obedient to your role requirements as a wife.

1. Be obedient to the words you state, as a confession or agreement.

Poor communication hampers even the best of marriages. A wife should "police" her conversation with her husband. If you have promised to do something, do it; or tell him you either need more time, you changed your mind, or it would be difficult for you to accomplish the task alone.

Be obedient to what you say with your mouth. The role of the wife is to be the *helper* and obey the boss (husband) so that the husband can obey his boss, Jesus Christ. The marriage is only as strong as its weakest link. Let it not be our link. Proverbs 21:23 says, "He who guards his mouth and his tongue, guards his soul from troubles."

You may disagree with your husband's wishes, suggestions, or commands. Be forthright with your words in the agreements and disagreements you make to your husband. When a wife is honest in her speech, a bond of integrity and trust interweave the hearts of a husband and a wife. Perhaps you are better at keeping your word than your husband keeps his. Correct him in love and not in discipline. Your patience may be tested, especially if your husband is a repeat offender. Remember the "70x7 rule," when Peter was asking Jesus how many times he was to forgive someone—seven times? And the Lord Jesus said, "no, 70x7." (See Matthew18: 21–22.) Meaning, the number of times one is to forgive another, is never ending. Consistency of positive words and truthful affirmations spoken will work to your favor when trying to help your husband cure his negative mouth.

Joy's Story

While dating my future husband, we would often meet at a parking area, closer to the lake, leave my car to journey on in his car with his boat in tow for a day of water skiing. I was driving a bright "apple green" older Toyota car passed onto me from my parents. (They knew I had to sell my more fashionable car to put the cash into my under-capitalized lingerie shop.) I remember one time, while getting gasoline, the young man cleaning my window on this "apple green baby" asked if this was my car. I said, "Yes," and he replied, "You sure don't look like you belong in this car." Though I was flattered by the compliment, I was very grateful for the transportation this gift provided me.

Every time Michael returned me to my car in the parking area he would say, "There's the green bomb!" I would softly retort "There's the green chariot" and we would laugh. After a summer of this, as we were once again approaching my car, I tightened my grip on the door handle to brace myself for his negative statement and to strengthen my courage for my follow-up retort, when to my surprise I heard Michael say, "there's the green chariot." I never said a word. I just smiled to myself. Several years after we were married I recounted this story to Michael. He never remembered making the change in his statement about my "apple green baby." He never remembered calling it the Green Chariot. I was convinced I was onto something powerful, and I became an avid policeman of my mouth from that day forth. Reading Proverbs has also strengthened my conviction of the power given to our spoken words.

Your words as his wife carry no authority to change your marriage. The husband's words carry that authority from God. But you can influence that "rainmaker" in your life. Watch your words, guard your mouth, bless and don't curse. Watch how and what you agree to with your mouth. If out of agreement with your husband's statement, restate your position to be in line with the obedience of your heart and God's Word. Make sure your husband has a clear understanding on where you stand with all the issues that could influence your life together, your marriage, and your persona.

Husbands seldom bother to figure out vague, indirect approaches. The clear bottom line conversations work best in making your points understood, with less emotional drama on your communication technique. Husbands often feel they are set-up when tears come. Pretend you are dating and want to make a good first impression, be thoughtful and kind in your obedience. Husbands listen better with this approach.

> The tongue of the wise makes knowledge acceptable, but the mouth of fools spouts folly.
>
> —PROVERBS 15:2

Short of being an abused wife on the run, *never lie to your husband*, even if he lies to you. This is for you! Don't ever lie to your husband. Otherwise, you are serving the "father of lies"—Satan. Lies are always self-serving and manipulative. It will cost you in the end, big time. If you have lied to your husband, seek his forgiveness and let him know of your sorrow and repentance. You may have to ask him to hold you accountable to regain his trust.

Wives who lie to their husbands also find it easy to lie to God and then wonder why they lack His favor. Proverb 19:5 states, "A false witness will not go unpunished, and he who tells lies will not escape."

Ecclesiastes 10:20 says, "Furthermore, in your bedchamber do not curse a king [husband or person of authority over your life]...for the bird of the heavens [angel] will carry the sound, and the winged creature will make the matter known." Amen.

If your husband lies—pray for him. I am particularly fond of "The Nathan Prayer." I tried it out on myself first.

Joy's Story—The Nathan Prayer

My mother had a stroke. She was in a nursing home adjacent to the assisted living care facility for my elderly father. My sister, Ann, and I traveled often to South Florida to visit our parents and to give our other two sisters in Florida a break.

These trips, an eleven-hour car trip, over a period of four years were always filled with non-stop laughter and robust conversation. Ann and I never ran out of subjects to discuss, debate, and analyze. Midway in this four-year period, I was becoming bolder and bolder with God to "clean me up," "show me my sin in my heart," "leave not a stone unturned." (By the way, I suggest that you do not pray this prayer unless you are ready for the rebukes that follow.) Unknowingly, my sister, Ann, did not understand why our trips to Florida had become more argumentative, with me confessing an issue buried in my heart, and asking Ann's forgiveness for a judgment, action, or sin. On one of the trips, I confessed to her that I was praying that God would send me a Nathan to rebuke me like he did King David. God took me at my word and, unfortunately, my "Nathan" was my sister Ann.

With many debates over our concern for the wellness and harmony of our relationship, I vowed to my sister Ann never to pray that prayer on any future trips or outings with her. I can still see Annie waving her finger at me before letting me in her car on those future trips to Florida. She held me accountable, and I love her for that.

How powerful is this prayer? My heart was open for godly rebuke, and Father God went deep. The heart surgery was a success, but the patient is still recovering, learning day by day about the consequences of being out of God's will and favor.

You may want to ask God to raise up a Nathan for your husband, who will rebuke him of all the ungodly things he is doing in your marriage. You should add to the prayer that God give your husband ears to hear, a heart to understand, and a desire to change. It's in God's hands. He knows what is best for your husband. Perhaps this will be an ongoing prayer until you see results or until God changes your prayer. God is for harmony, peace, and passion in your marriage.

I have heard it said that the more spiritual spouse would apologize first. Reflect on this. However, the more spiritual spouse should not use their spiritual gifts as a weapon. Remember, what comes out of your husband's mouth can change your life totally. Let us be wise about how to approach our husbands with truth. Proverbs 21:21 says, "He who pursues righteousness and loyalty finds life, righteousness and honor."

2. Be obedient to the Word of God

Some wives who are frustrated in their marriages call themselves "Christians, " and yet are not faithfully reading the Word of God. That's like a woman in a boat who fails to bring the oars, yet expects a miracle from God to reach her destination. When we are struggling in our marriage, the answers to all our questions can be found in His Word. Causal, random reading of God's Word would be a poor option. Diligence brings about change and freedom. Proverbs 16:20 says, "He who gives attention to the word will find good, and blessed is he who trusts in the Lord."

The Book of Genesis offers stories of relationships and God's power in the lives of those early couples. They understood the consequences of disobedience, and were able to see the fruits of their choices.

Why is this so different a picture in today's Christian marriages? The answer is, lack of knowledge. You can't become obedient to God's Word if you don't know it. Let us be wise women and seek the Word of God. Read one book of Proverbs—one for each day of the month. These chapters make excellent bedtime reading, as we fill our mind with His Word as we slip into bed. Proverbs 23:12, "Apply your heart to discipline, and your ears to words of knowledge."

As an obedient helper, familiarize yourself with God's rules and His requirements of you in this role. Obedience, once learned and embraced, brings sweet rewards. Remember, obedience to your husband is for *your* protection and safety.

3. Be obedient to your role-requirements as wife

Caution is the word for wives that step in front of their husbands and think they are helping. Perhaps his mother did the same as he grew up. Perhaps you think you can "kick start" your husband into being a better husband, lover, or provider with a little more aggression on your part. Must God have to keep up with two disobedient spouses before He can operate in your marriage?

"Why not be wronged for Christ sake," (See 1 Cor. 6:7), has never been a favorite scripture of mine, yet I have learned great obedience through it. This obedience has become a consistent safeguard over my life. I now enjoy a sweet rest in its provision.

You are unique and cherished by God. Trust God's love and let Him fight your battles. After all, He knows the motives in the heart of your enemy, which may very well be yourself. Proverbs14:1 states, "The wise woman builds her house, but the foolish tears it down with her own hands."

A beautiful scripture verse exhorts us to embrace godly obedience.

"Obey your leaders and submit to them; for they keep watch over your souls, as those who will give an account. Let them do this with joy and not with grief, for this would be unprofitable for you," Hebrews 13:17. Amen.

We women are designed by God to be obedient. Therefore, He requires it. That mantel of peace and safety we embrace in our marriage is the fruit of this obedience.

Respect—The Wife's Role

When defining the word *respect*, we find that it means to esteem high or special regard, or deserving of high regard as defined by *Webster's Dictionary*. Therefore, "to respect" does not mean, "to admire" and this could be where some of the conflict about respecting our husband gets misunderstood. The "deserving of high regard" could convince one that respect is earned. But a respectful posture is a choice. It is a choice a wife can make. This does not necessarily mean that you "admire" your husband, but that you are respectful of his position of authority over your life. 1 Peter 3:2 says, "as they [husbands] observe your [wife's] chaste and respectful behavior."

Knowing that respect is earned, consequently, respect cannot demand to have its own way. Respect cannot demand submission. Respect cannot be a negotiating tool in arguments. Respect is the earned response from the actions and words of the person seeking respect—the husband. Respect will need to be earned if it is to achieve a heartfelt response. No one wants to be respected in a "rote" tone of voice. Your husband wants you to respect him and to admire his efforts. Most husbands want their wife's respect to be an irrevocable heart condition with an unconditional response clause. Unfortunately, we live in a fallen world with daily changes to the dynamics in our lives, which are complicated by the consequences of our choices. This makes unconditional respect a daily challenge.

A respectful attitude toward your husband is not built on his success or failure at earning your respect, but by your respectful demeanor shown in respecting his position of authority over your life, and his position of responsibility for your well-being. A respectful attitude will keep the peace and the conflict issues to a minimum in your marriage. Therefore a respectful attitude does not mean you need to be 100 percent in agreement with your husband's wishes. You are still able and encouraged to voice your opinion in a respectful manner.

More people know the definition of respect by its *absence* and not so much by its presence. It is not the wife's place to be the judge for earned respect. It could prove to be self-serving or manipulative. Let the bar of your husband's earned respect be set to God's standards—His Word.

It's a reflection of great character and honor for a wife to *be* respectful of her husband. God has purposed and planned for His brides to be respectful and charming. How you treat your husband—respectfully or disrespectfully—is a reflection of how much Jesus you have in your heart. I struggled with this lesson but learned that it gets easier as God's truth takes root in my heart. Ephesians 5:21 says, "and be subject to one another in the fear [respect] of Christ."

If respect was abused in your family when you were growing up, or misused as a weapon by your mother, or absent altogether, you will be challenged as to its proper place in your relationship with your husband. And if your husband came from the same dysfunction in his family, it compounds the problem. Argumentative disharmony would be a mild description of the emotional stress in your marriage.

You did accept your husband's marriage proposal—right? Surely your "yes" to his proposal wasn't based on infatuation and promises. Well then, you are stuck with your choice, which carries with it a *limited-exception clause*.

This *limited-exception clause* would include physical, verbal, and emotional abuse against you by your husband; as well as, adultery that is physical—the actual act of sex, or emotional—engaging in lustful pursuits.

Matthew 5:28 says, "but I [Jesus] say to you, that everyone who looks at a woman to lust for her has committed adultery with her already in his heart." Therefore, this would also include a husband's sin with pornography and spiritual adultery.

Your husband has to be of some value and merit for you to have married him. If you find it hard to respect your husband, as a husband or as a man, then you will have to formulate a game plan, orchestrated by God, to draw your husband to a place of hearing truth and taking action.

Most husbands desire to be their wife's "prince." His actions may not match his heart. Perhaps you are convinced that he will never see you as his "princess," but are you acting like a princess? I have been there. It took my husband ten years to call me by a cherished name. He came up with princess on his own. It changed to godly princess in the later days of his life. Michael wanted to be my hero, and I had to learn to let him—even if he didn't hit all the hit marks on *my* hero's report card. 2 Corinthians 2:2 states, "For if I cause you sorrow, who then makes me glad but the one whom I made sorrowful."

Yes, respect is earned. Likely you are waiting for your husband to *win* your respect. It may never come on your terms. But you can help your husband in his struggle to respect you as a woman. 1 Peter 3:7 says, "You husbands likewise, live with your wives in an understanding way, as with a weaker vessel, since she is a woman."

Perhaps your husband didn't respect his mother, as a woman, for a number of reasons. Possibly his father didn't respect her either. The list can be long, but the answer is short—*prayer.*

Respect is a position of *grace*. The same grace our heavenly Father gives us daily. This posture of grace is the posture of a princess. We are all Father God's "princess." Let us claim our inheritance and practice the posture of a princess.

A description of a godly princess:

Proverbs 11:16: "A gracious woman attains honor."

Proverbs 31:25: "Strength and dignity are her clothing and she smiles at the future.

Every wife can and should be her husband's princess. Perhaps with a little princess training, you could find yourself holding court with your beloved prince (*charming* would be a plus, but it is still optional). How do I know you are his princess and that he is your prince? Proverbs 31:10 says, "An excellent wife, who can find? For her worth is far above jewels." Proverbs 12:4 states, "An excellent [virtuous] wife is the *crown* of her husband." Remember it is to our honor to act as a princess and be called a princess, if not by our husband, by God.

This may appear all too simple amidst the pain, rejection, anger, and loneliness you may be encountering in your marriage. But the choice is ours; the reaction is ours, and the action ours. There is hope. There is healing. There is renewal. There is reward. There is prayer!

When a husband seems unaware or unappreciative of our respectful attitude toward him, and complaining and yelling have failed, try prayer. Give God room to operate, and give your angels a mission to fulfill. For they oversee His Word to perform it. Let your requests be made known to Father God through the intercession of our Savior and Lord, Jesus Christ. Psalm 116:1–2 says, "I love the

Lord, because He hears my voice and my supplications. Because He has inclined His ear to me, therefore I shall call upon Him as long as I live."

A prayer of wisdom for your husband

Ephesians 1:17–19, "That the God of our Lord Jesus Christ, the Father of glory, may give to _____ (husband's name) a spirit of wisdom and of revelation in the knowledge of God. I pray that the eyes of _____ (husband's name) heart may be enlightened, so that _____ (husband's name) may know what is the hope of God's calling. What are the riches of the glory of God's inheritance in _____ (husband's name) who believes."

I ask Father God in the name of Jesus, that my husband _____ (husband's name) will have a heart that trusts in me. He will live with me in understanding and with knowledge and grant me honor because I am a woman." Amen.

This is not a one-time prayer. It took me a season to believe that the words of this petition could actually be fulfilled. To pray, believing is a powerful stronghold! Don't wait too long to pray this prayer. Time can be your enemy that says, "He'll never change—why waste your time."

Some women wonder why their husbands treat them like their fathers treated their mothers. Was your father unkind, dishonoring, and unaffectionate to your mother? Perhaps you had a father who did not cleave to your mother, and therefore, your mother's reactions were over-the-top. You might have said, "I'll never marry a man like my father." Or, "I'll never marry a man who treats me like my father treats my mother." Or, perhaps you were daddy's little girl and didn't understand spiritual adultery, which is when your father gives the love, care, and attention to you, that belonged to your mother. Where is the end to unraveling these dysfunctional events in our childhood? Proverbs 2:6 tells us, "For the Lord gives wisdom; from His mouth comes knowledge and understanding."

Knowledge, truth, and honesty—bring freedom! All are needed so we can walk through that door into God's freedom and with it, become equipped to fulfill His purpose in our life. The purpose of life cannot be to focus on our husband's faults and problems, nor can it be to live in denial of the loneliness in our marriage and call it "living for God." God is not impressed with such self-sacrifice. God requires obedience rather than sacrifice.

So what is the key to the knowledge, truth, and honesty that will set you on a course to freedom? Could this be your statement of truth? "To tell you the truth, I am hurting in my marriage. And I am honestly seeking God's knowledge to bring myself in line with God's will as a Christian wife who *can* respect her husband." This is a starting place. If you are unhappy with your husband and lonely due to his lack of holding you in a position of honor and his lack of genuine affection and passion, and you call all *this* by the right name—you have a shot at freedom.

But if you say, "I have to consider the children. He's a good provider; he's a kind husband; we do take vacations; he's a good friend; he's a Christian and takes us to church each week; he volunteers for Christian activities"—stop! This is not the picture of the "heartfelt, intimate marriage" relationship that Father God wants for us. Jesus says, "that a husband is to cherish and nourish his wife." (See Ephesians 5:28–29.) Cherish and nourish are *not* words that appear in 1 Corinthians13 where agape love is defined. Cherish and nourish are words of passion between a husband and wife—not between Dad and the kids or Mom and the kids.

Denial is an unfaithful friend. It leads us to believe that living in a lonely marriage for the sake of the children pleases God. Let's understand the Word of God. There is nowhere I've found, in the Word of God, that a parent is to choose the child over the spouse—nowhere. There is nowhere in the Word where parents are *"rewarded"* by God for how well they nurture or cherish their children. However it does say:

> Fathers, do not provoke your children to anger.
> —EPHESIANS 6:4

> Fathers, do not exasperate your children, so that they will not lose heart.
> —COLOSSIANS 3:21

The husband and wife will be rewarded according to their marriage relationship with each other. The husband, especially, will give an account to God on how well he took care of his bride (wife), emotionally, spiritually, and physically. Ephesians 5:25–27 says, "Husbands, love your wives, just as Christ also loved the church and gave Himself up for her, so that He might sanctify her, having cleansed her by the washing of water with the word, that He might present to Himself the church in all her glory, having no spot or wrinkle or any such thing; but that she should be holy and blameless." What will his report card look like? You can help him by being honest in your relationship with him.

If there is a lack of respect between husband and wife, this is often missing in their relationship with Father God. Or, it could be from judging your parents and reaping that judgment in your own marriage, as stated in Romans 2:1, "Every one of you who passes judgment, for in that which you judge another, you condemn yourself... and [will] practice the same thing?"

There is a price for freedom. It starts with an honest evaluation of your relationship with your husband, speaking truth to your spouse; then arming yourself with the knowledge of God's Word and applying it to the challenges in your marriage. This truth will fashion a marriage worthy of God's blessing. In doing this, you have given God permission to operate in your marriage—starting with you.

The following prayer can help those, who by judging their father's and/or mother's behavior in their marriage, find the *same* dysfunctional dance of disrespect and lack of honor operating in their own marriage.

First comes *honesty*, "Yes, I judged my mother/or father's marriage."

Second comes *truth*, "Yes, I have the same dynamics going on in my marriage."

Third come *knowledge*, "Yes, I will confess God's Word, repent, ask forgiveness and trust in God's deliverance."

Do not say this prayer if you are stuck on any of the first, second, or third points. It will sound *rote* and will frustrate your results. You may choose to keep your marriage as it is, finding the pain is a more familiar companion than the unknown companion of freedom.

You have probably carried too much of the emotional load in your marriage already in "raising" your husband, and this would just be added to your list of responsibilities. Please don't discount God. He really is bigger than the enemy operating in your lonely marriage.

Prayer for judging parents

"Most gracious and Holy Father God, in the name of my Savior and Lord, Jesus Christ, I ask that your forgive me for all the many times I judged my _____ (father and/or mother) and their marriage. Forgive me for all the many times I said, "I will never marry a man like my father." Forgive me for all the many times I judged my mother and said in my heart, "I'll never have a marriage like my mother's." I continue to seek your favor, Father God, as I repent for having made these judgments of my parents. I ask you, Father God, in the name of Jesus and by your grace, to annul the consequences that would fall to me because of these judgments; and to also annul the consequences of my judgments, which have defiled my husband and defiled my marriage." Amen.

"Father God, I forgive my _____ (father and/or mother) for all the emotional hardship, anger, and disharmony I endured in my family unit in my formative years. I forgive you father for _____, _____, _____, (anger, rage, indiffer-

ence, lack of affection, fear), which caused me to be anxious and untrusting of men in general. And mother, I forgive you for _____, _____, _____ (nagging, yelling, controlling, fear), and actions in our home that caused strife.

"Father God, I ask that you forgive my parents for all the ways they harmed me emotionally by their actions toward me and by their _____ (harsh or indifferent actions) between themselves, I ask all this in Jesus' name." Amen.

"Father God, I ask in the name of Jesus, that you would do a new work in my heart and destroy all the inner vows I made to protect myself from marrying someone like my father—even the vows I made that I wanted to marry someone like my father. Take out my heart of stone and give me a heart of flesh—create in me a clean heart and renew a right spirit in me." Amen.

"Father God, forgive me for all the many times I showed disrespect to my parents, in anger. Forgive me for showing this same disrespect to my husband _____. Forgive me for all the many times I have harmed my husband emotionally with my disrespect and restore his heart to self-respect with an overwhelming presence of Your love, I ask this in Jesus' name." Amen.

You may also want to directly ask your husband for forgiveness for the disrespect you have shown him. This cycle of forgiveness in your marriage could start with you.

These prayers are your petitions before Father God through the Lord Jesus Christ to intervene on your behalf. Change any of the words or phrases in these prayers to best reflect the challenges in your marriage. These need to be *your* prayers.

How long will you have to repeat these prayers? Until you see results or get, a release in your spirit. I have come to enjoy this time of intimate honesty when making my petition to Father God because He always listens. Psalms 4:3 says, "The Lord hears when I call to Him."

Summary—Wife

The challenging questions in my own troublesome marriage left me wondering if it wasn't all me. Should I quit and call the environment in my marriage by a name that would validate my existence? With no children to cushion my loneliness I was totally awake to the daily presence of my aloneness. Part of me felt concern that I would become accustomed to my loneliness and view life through apathetic eyes. I shuddered at that thought and became motivated to find God's answers. I refused to quit. I refused to settle for a lie. I refused to take the path of less resistance. My mission was for truth and with God's guidance I knew I could find it.

Believe God for miracles in your marriage. The rewards will make your journey to freedom worth the effort and will build in you spiritual muscles of knowledge and wisdom, far more valuable than gold or silver.

You now know God's rules for wives to achieve success in your marriage. The wife is her husband's helper/companion, who desires intimacy with him and is subject to his leadership. Embraced with an attitude (*the roles*) of an honest responder, with an obedient and a respectful posture, you will ensure a strong position for pleasing God. Once we women get right with God, God moves on the hearts of our husbands. That's a promise from Him. God looks out for His brides. Malachi 2:14 says, "The Lord has been a witness between you and the wife of your youth, against whom you have dealt treacherously, though she is your companion and your wife by covenant."

If at any point in your challenging marriage and open discussions with your husband, your communication is clouded with unresolved conflict and negative childhood issues that continue to sabotage your quest for truth, Christian marital counseling may be an appropriate option. Find the right Christian counselor. Ask questions. Ask for references where possible. Your husband should also be part of this quest. Keep in mind that the Christian counselor will *only* guide you and your husband to truth. The work to be done in your heart is up to you. In addition, seek God's guidance through reverent prayer and unhurried listening. He has much to share with you.

After all, you are His Princess! And He loves you passionately with an everlasting love.

Part V

Rewards

Father is the One who impartially judges according to each one's work, conduct yourselves in fear during the time of your stay on earth.

—1 Peter 1:17

Chapter 12

Gain and Loss

W E ALL LIKE THE word *rewards*! It makes us imagine the soon coming gifts of a job well done. Often we wonder when these rewards are achieved—here or in heaven. Why are rewards appropriate in a book about marriages? Let us consider what and why rewards are important, from our standpoint and from God's.

> The one who despises the word will be in debt to it, but the one who fears the commandment will be rewarded.
> —PROVERBS 13:13

What is God really conveying here in the above scripture?

Webster's Dictionary defines despise as disdain; detest; regard as negligible, worthless, or distasteful.

The word *despise* almost carries with it an aroma of rebellion. And with this rebellion comes *loss of reward.* On the other hand, one who respects and carries out the command of God's holy Word will, by its nature, bring a *gain of reward.* So where's the problem? The problem is that we don't like God telling us "what to do" and "how to do it." Smells like rebellion.

Why should we care about rewards? Because, our journey as a married spouse is, in part, designed to help us clean up our act. The sanctification process—if you will. "Iron sharpens iron, so one man sharpens another" (Prov. 27:17). There is not a more intimate place than marriage to go deep into the heart and plumb the depth of our being.

Sometimes what comes *up* and *out* of our heart, by route of our vocal cords, isn't loving, kind, life giving, encouraging, or honoring. If we want to know how well we are doing, listen to our talk, especially to our spouse. This is when the real test of what is in our heart comes. It's easy to be kind and thoughtful to a stranger, yet dishonor our spouse with words of unkindness. Unkind words toward our spouse quickly become a forgotten memory. Except for God's bookkeeping system, which states, "Every careless word you utter, you will be held accountable." Even though you did go out of your way to do a good deed for a stranger, Jesus says, "And I say to you, that every careless word that men shall speak, they shall render account for it in the 'day of judgment.' For by your words you shall be justified, and by your words you shall be condemned" (Matt. 12:36–37).

Let's be clear on this point, God does not need *our* approval on how well He is doing. We do! The gain or loss of rewards is an eternal proposition, which will last forever!

There are some points that need to be understood and internalized to best comprehend why rewards are important to God and therefore, should be important to us. I never like to assume I have a clearer understanding of my life in eternity with rewards hanging in balance.

Understanding God's reward system is best illustrated by His Word.

> And inasmuch as it is appointed for men to die once and after this comes judgment.
>
> —HEBREWS 9:27

For we shall all stand before the judgment seat of God.
—ROMANS 14:10

For we must all appear before the judgment seat of Christ that each one may be recompensed [loss or gain of rewards] for his deeds in the body, according to what he has done, whether good or bad.
—2 CORINTHIANS 5:10

If any man's work which he has built upon remains, he will receive a reward.
—1 CORINTHIANS 3:14

Beware of practicing your righteousness before men to be noticed by them; otherwise you have no reward with your Father who is in heaven.
—MATTHEW 6:1

We know our journey does not end with our physical death on plant earth. Our journey of life with Father God, the Lord Jesus, the Holy Spirit, our ministering angels and our saved loved ones will continue. However our deeds, actions, and choices of obedience or disobedience to His Word will mark out for us, and will establish our unchangeable eternal address in heaven.

For married couples, Father God makes clear his position as to how well we took advantage of the purging process, which comes with married life. This individual sanctification process in marriage is deep and life changing, for eternity. Therefore, rewards and loss of rewards are not given to us as a couple, but for our individual performance.

In 1 Corinthians 3:8, Paul said, "Now he who plants and he who waters are one [husband and wife—joint efforts]; but each will receive his own reward according to his own labor." I believe that could be one reason we are not married in heaven, since each spouse will have a different mansion address, depending on the level of our individual rewards. (It would be nice though, to be in the same neighborhood.) But Jesus answered and said to them, "You are mistaken, not understanding the Scriptures nor the power of God. For in the resurrection they [married spouses] neither marry nor are given in marriage, but are like angels in heaven" (Matt. 22:29–30).

This is where a hearing tune-up would be advantageous to better comprehend your spouse's honest report of your performance in the marriage. How many times did you tell your spouse, "I can never please you," to keep any further rebuke or correction at arm's length? Or, "Stop making me feel guilty; look at yourself, little self-righteous." Statements like these prevent the purging in a heart of rebellion, which is really rebellion against God. Better here, than there. Once we step over the line into eternity and taste His sweet love and forgiveness, it leaves us powerless to change our account balance with Father God. Let us be wise in knowing that this life is but a hand breadth, and we are but a vapor. We have only a short time to work out the rebellion in our hearts. So, grab you spouse right now and say, "I want to hear *everything*!" It will pay big dividends in your eternal investment program.

Let us address some causes to loss of rewards. In 1 Corinthians 3:15, apostle Paul said, "If any man's work is burned up, he will suffer loss; but he himself will be saved, yet so as through fire." Paul is directing us to test our "works" before God to see if our choices *here* line up for rewards *there*. Remember, where your heart is—so is your treasure. If you make poor choices here, that cause a loss of rewards there, that is unfortunate. Even so, you will not lose your salvation and rightful passage into heaven; although you will miss out on those nice rewards you could be enjoying forever and perhaps a really nice mansion to brighten your homecoming. Who said God wasn't into details? In John 14:2, Jesus comforts His disciples, saying, "In My Father's house are many dwelling places; if it were not so, I would have told you; for I go to prepare a place for you."

There is no "redo" once we have stepped into eternity. What we choose to do with our life here, our choices, behavior, and beliefs travel with us forever and will forever define our future.

The process of purging can be slow and painful, and last the length of our journey here. God, in His perfect timing, allows us to experience the consequences of our free-will choices. Those choices reflect our heart's condition. It is not always a pretty picture, but we learn that obedience is better then sacrifice.

Psalm 51:16 says, "For you do not delight in sacrifice, otherwise I would give it." It is important to know that this is one of the measuring rods that God uses to grade our behavior. Are you obedient, without whining, about His commandments and laws, or do you mess up and then try to "sand-bag" God with your pious behavior of sacrifice? God is not impressed. Proverbs 17:3 states, "the Lord tests hearts."

In 1 Corinthians 6:9–10, "Do not be deceived; neither fornicators, nor idolaters, nor adulterers, nor effeminate, nor homosexuals, not thieves, nor the covetous, nor drunkards, nor revilers, nor swindlers, shall inherit [a reward in] the Kingdom of God." These sin issues that are not dealt with, will cause you to lose reward—eternally. The wages of sin is death. God reads the motives of our hearts; because our actions carry with it, its own gain or loss of reward here.

Galatians 6:7 says, "Do not be deceived, God is not mocked; for whatever a man sows, this he will also reap."

If your heart entertains any of these sin conditions, know that once you acknowledge this sin; confessed this as *your* sin; seeking Father God's forgiveness; then repent and be healed. God has a permanent eraser that will wipe this sin off your *page* of remembrance. Amen. Also beware, just because you have stopped participating in any of the above sin issues, but yet your heart is still posed with a passion for that sin, means you have not conquered your sin. God still *sees* it as unrighteousness in your heart, because it has the authority to overpower you to sin once again. God reads the motives of the heart to determine righteousness.

Jesus speaking in Matthew 5:28, said "but I say to you, that everyone who looks at a woman [or male] to lust for her [or him] has committed adultery with her [or him] in his heart." If in your attempt to neutralize this sin in your heart, through "righteous activities" for God, don't—it is really nauseating to Him. He is very black and white; don't look to the right or left but look unto Me; let your yes be yes and your no be no.

He knows which ones are His. We may fool the world with dazzling conversations, fine grooming, or successes, but God is not fooled. It adds up to dust in our hands at life's end if we haven't allowed God to do His heart surgery on our sin issues and remove the veil from our eyes. It says in Proverbs 17:10, "A rebuke goes deeper into one who has understanding than a hundred blows into a fool." And Proverbs 26:12 says, "Do you see a man wise in his own eyes? There is more hope for a fool than for him." Let us not be foolish. Time's passage does not automatically erase sin issues in our heart. With time, however, it becomes harder to believe we still have the sin issue, especially if we have adjusted our life to accommodate its existence. And by this—we become the fool.

There is a check and balance system, which helps us keep a short account of the needed changes in our heart, thoughts, actions, and behaviors. "But if we judged ourselves rightly, we would not be judged" (1 Cor. 11:31). The apostle Paul asks us to wake up, take an inventory of our lives, and become accountable for our actions and words because they will come back to bless or curse us. Let us have ears to hear. There is danger of betrayal in marriages that appear, as calming placid waters to the observer and even to some family members, while underneath are violent undertows and death of your call and purpose from God. Aren't you glad that the gain of rewards and the loss of rewards are rated fairly by God? By the way, ignorance or lack of knowledge of God's measuring stick for rewards will not negate the final results.

Take comfort in this, that in reading this book you are in a better position to make the needed changes that are in line with His teachings and hence, His rewards. Having read this book, I must again warn you that you are accountable before Him for *now* knowing this truth in His Word. James 4:17 says (emphasis added), "Therefore, to the one who knows the *right thing to do*, and does not do it, to him it is sin." Each day that you know your actions, attitudes, or behaviors are not in line with God's teaching, you are sinning. Everyday that you disobey, it is accounted to you as sin; and you will continue to lose reward. This daily loss of reward, due to sin, will also cancel out rewards earned from righteous behavior in other areas of your life.

God's bookkeeping system is simple and straightforward. We can't have it both ways, like living "half saved."

For those who are still embracing deep-rooted sin as a way of life, God desires that we be grieved in our spirit. Whatever sin we embrace in our heart, which has convinced our mind that keeping the sin a secret carries with it a bigger reward of self-protection and self-enhancement, than God's eternal reward—is believing a lie! God knows every detail of your sin, and the trophy of His rewards can only be compared to the sweet taste of freedom He provides to those who seek Him with a heart of permanent repentance. God can make that permanent repentance a reality in any life. How? He knows the "root" of our sin; and knows its name.

To our husbands—you are challenged everyday in your job with gains and losses. How can this be so different? Yes, it will require a change of heart and a change of perspective, but it carries with it the many rewards of obedience. Remember—God holds the husband 100 percent accountable for the success or failure of the marriage. His Word does not allow debate about the rules and roles in a Christian marriage. You have more responsibility, which carries with it more rewards and losses than your wife. She's a reflection of you and your actions, as a man and husband, on how well your "raised" her in the garden of your marriage.

Time will not change God's mind and allow you to treat your wife poorly, under *any* circumstance. Nor does your wife's unkind response to you change God's decision of your accountability. God gave the husband godly authority to handle well his marriage and the intimacy with his wife. If any of this is not working, continue to re-read the Husband section of this book until you understand why your intimacy with your wife does not honor or reflect God.

Your intimacy or lack of intimacy with your wife reflects directly your closeness and intimacy with God. He is grieved over the childhood issues that scarred your heart. God also had to watch His own Son take nasty blows and false acquisitions for us, thus providing a way of escape from the lies you came to believe about yourself. He has provided the cross.

It's reward time. It is time to get serious and hand off those silly toys and grab God's truth and let it soak into every cell of your being. Let it transform your heart, your mind, your thoughts, and your actions. God made His men strong and courageous. Stand up to your full stature as a man and claim your prize—your reward.

Some of us will receive "crowns" along with our rewards. How magnificent is that! Hebrews 10:35–36 says, "Therefore do not throw away your confidence, which has a great reward. For you have need of endurance, so that when you have done the will of God, you may receive what was promised." James 1:12 states, "Blessed is a man who perseveres under trail; for once he has been approved, he will receive the crown of life which the Lord has promised to those who love Him." Ruth 2:11–12 tells us, "May the Lord reward your work."

God has ordained our time of birth (Ps. 139:16); He gave us "gifts" (Rom. 11:29); and He gave us a desire to do what is right and holy (Prov. 2:10). Each person's journey has its own set of challenges and choices that will shape one's concept of God and His righteousness. He has prepared a place for us to live with Him forever—a promise. A promise of salvation for all those who have received His Son, the Lord Jesus Christ, as their personal Savior, will have eternal life and a chance to receive rewards. These rewards are everlasting and are given in heaven to His saved "people."

My late husband, Michael, is in his white robe embracing rewards of a man who ran his race well, who prostrated his heart before the throne of God for rebuke and healing. Michael's heart seeking contrition and forgiveness has found favor with God, a job well done, Michael.

As born-again believers, we all carry in our hearts the promise of Revelation 22:12, "Behold I am coming quickly, and My reward is with Me, to render to every man according to what he has done." Amen.

Notes

The definitions presented throughout the book are from *Merriam-Webster's Collegiate Dictionary, Eleventh Edition* (Springfield, MA: Merriam-Webster, 2003).

Introduction

1. Statistical data found at website: http://www.cdc.gov/nchs/fastats/divorce.htm (accessed November 5, 2010).

Chapter 6
Rules: Immutable Laws, Unchanging

1. Statistics found at website: http://www.aakp.org/aakp-library/anemia-kidney-disease/ (accessed November 5, 2010).

2. Recalled from memory of a presentation Pastor Wright gave at a church in Peachtree City, Georgia, in 1999.

Chapter 7
Roles: Attitude of the Heart

1. Gordon Dalbey, *Healing the Masculine Soul* (Nashville, TN: Thomas Nelson, 2003).

Chapter 8
Rules: Cleave, Authority, Provide

1. Quote recalled from a financial lectures tape series titled *Investment Principles*, by Larry Burkett of Christian Financial Concepts.

Chapter 9
Roles: Love, Honor, Protect
Physical Protection

1. Physical characteristics unique to males and females, from Focus On the Family website, http://family.custhelp.com/app/answers/detail/a_id/1086/~/could-you-list-the-physical-characteristics-unique-to-males-and-females%3F (accessed November 5, 2010).

About the Author

THE JOURNEY IN WRITING this book has left me wanting more of Him. Trying to understand God's truth, in all areas of life, is my desired quest. Presently, I am waiting for my next move at His leading. God's plans have always been perfect for me. Knowing that without His anointing, any venture promoted by self would be pure folly. Therefore, I have learned to walk a little slower and embrace each day with thankfulness.

My passion is to speak into the heart of the listener the truths set forth in this book, with a desire to reach a wide variety of audience groups and variety of age groups with this marital guide. This information is vital for navigating through the rough, choppy waters of marital struggle and/or preparing to dealing with issues prior to that walk down the aisle. I have made myself available for Christian TV and radio, churches, women's groups, Christian counseling seminars, and Christian Colleges and Universities, to name a few. For more information on my speaking schedule or to request my availability, I can be contacted at 800-705-9958 or through my website at www.growinhealth.com or email at callahan@growinhealth.com.

Being widowed in November 2007 has placed me at God's side, giving me a peaceful sense of His watchful care over my life. So for right now, I am content with all that He has planned for my future.

Enjoy the journey and cherish your visit.

Grow in Health Ministry

"A seed of truth produces an ongoing harvest of freedom."
—Joy Callahan, founder

Our ministry is designed and inspired by Father God to reach the lost, the backslider, and the challenged redeemed. Along with writing for Him, He has prevailed upon me to make available the salvation bracelets I have designed and made for many years as gifts for family members and friends.

These personalized salvation bracelets are designed as a visible reminder of His ownership in our lives. Made using the finest Swarovski crystals, these brilliant multi-colored bracelets tell the story of our journey from salvation to streets of gold. They are personalized with sterling silver letters for names or initials surrounded by the owner's birthstone colored crystals.

Each bracelet is handmade by a devoted Christian.

> And they overcame him [the accuser of the brethren] because of the blood of the Lamb and because of the word of their testimony.
>
> —Revelation 12:11,
> Authors paraphrase

This salvation bracelet is our testimony of our life in Christ to everyone who sees it and is inspired by its message. It is a wonderful reflection of His love and providential plan for our future. They are available at: www.salvation-bracelets.com. This book is also under our ministry and can be ordered online @ www.joycallahan.com.

Enjoy!